UNDERSTANDING
URBAN GOVERNMENT

UNDERSTANDING URBAN GOVERNMENT

Metropolitan Reform Reconsidered

Robert L. Bish
Vincent Ostrom

American Enterprise Institute for Public Policy Research
Washington, D. C.

65701

Robert L. Bish is associate professor of economics and urban affairs
at the University of Southern California.

Vincent Ostrom is professor of political science at Indiana University.

ISBN 0-8447-3120-x

Domestic Affairs Study 20, December 1973

Second printing September 1974

Third printing, August 1975

Fourth printing, March 1976

Library of Congress Catalog Card No. L.C. 73-91114

Printed in the United States of America

. . . the ideas of economists and political philosophers, both when they are right and when they are wrong, are more powerful than is commonly understood. Indeed the world is ruled by little else. Practical men, who believe themselves to be quite exempt from any intellectual influences, are usually the slaves of some defunct economist. Madmen in authority, who hear voices in the air, are distilling their frenzy from some academic scribbler of a few years back. I am sure that the power of vested interests is vastly exaggerated compared with the gradual encroachment of ideas. Not, indeed, immediately but after a certain interval; for in the field of economic and political philosophy there are not many who are influenced by new theories after they are twenty-five or thirty years of age, so that the ideas which civil servants and politicians and even agitators apply to current events are not likely to be the newest. But, soon or late, it is ideas, not vested interests, which are dangerous for good or evil.

John Maynard Keynes

CONTENTS

65701

HIGHLIGHTS

(1) The contemporary urban crisis involves a "crisis of understanding" which casts substantial doubt upon our basic knowledge of how governmental institutions work.

(2) The traditional wisdom used to reform government in metropolitan areas presumes that fragmentation of authority and overlapping jurisdictions are the primary causes of urban ills. A single unit of government controlled by a few policy officials and administered by a single chief executive is considered to be the appropriate remedy.

(3) A new reform movement demanding community control and neighborhood government within large central cities challenges the basic concepts used in the traditional approach to metropolitan reform. Big city governments are viewed as unresponsive, cumbersome and inefficient.

(4) A new approach to understanding government is being developed by a number of political economists who apply economic reasoning to public sector problems. These political economists use a mode of analysis similar to that used by James Madison, Alexander Hamilton and Alexis de Tocqueville. Their public choice approach offers a different explanation for how governmental institutions work.

(5) The public choice approach begins with *individuals*, considers the nature of *public goods and services* and explores how differently organized systems of urban government satisfy individual preferences for public goods and services.

(6) Different public goods and services are most efficiently provided under different organizational arrangements. Services which involve

proportionately large expenditures for physical facilities may be provided most efficiently by large organizations. Economies in such services can often be realized by serving large populations and large areas.

(7) Other services, such as education and police, are provided in person-to-person situations. These services are both more difficult to manage and highly sensitive to individual preferences and localized conditions. Diseconomies are likely to accrue when these services are organized on a large scale.

(8) A governmental system of multiple, overlapping jurisdictions can take advantage of diverse economies of scale for different public services. A public economy composed of multiple jurisdictions is likely to be more efficient and responsive than a public economy organized as a single area-wide monopoly.

(9) Intergovernmental relationships are especially important in a public economy composed of a multiplicity of overlapping governmental jurisdictions. Tax competition and coordination, fiscal transfers and service contracts can facilitate mutually productive intergovernmental cooperation. Courts, legislatures and informal arrangements are also available for the resolution of intergovernmental conflicts. Multiple agencies serving the same people with different bundles of public goods and services can be viewed as multiple firms in *public service industries*. Constrained competition between multiple "firms" operating in different public service industries can create relatively efficient and responsive systems of government in metropolitan areas.

(10) Empirical investigation of public sector activities casts substantial doubt upon the traditional wisdom used in proposing simple merger and consolidation of governments as the solution to urban problems. What evidence does exist indicates that alternative approaches and explanations are more realistic and offer better prospects for alleviating urban ills.

(11) Important items for future study of urban affairs include: (a) neighborhood governments, (b) multi-organizational structures, (c) public service contracting, (d) user charges, fiscal relations and income redistribution, (e) the legal architecture of complex governmental systems, (f) patterns of bureaucratic behavior, (g) relationships among officials, professionals and citizen-clients, and (h) new research strategies to improve our understanding of urban government.

2

1
THE URBAN CRISIS AND POLITICAL REFORM

Over the course of the last decade increasing attention has been given to critical problems arising from the frustrations of city life and the failure of city governments to cope with many of the elementary problems of everyday living. Simple tasks such as the removal of trash and garbage from public streets are not being satisfactorily discharged in large areas of the most densely populated sections of major cities. Street crimes are soaring. People are wary about venturing into public streets alone except during full daylight. The risk of crimes against person and property are too great to proceed without special precautions. Schools in many areas have become little more than custodial institutions. The poor drop out, and the well-to-do opt out, going to private or suburban schools. Whole neighborhoods have the appearance of being bombed out.

We wish to acknowledge the helpfulness of the following colleagues and readers who have offered numerous comments and suggestions: Frances Bish, James Buchanan, Virginia Fielder, John Hamilton, Thomas F. Johnson, Herbert Kiesling, Philip Kronenberg, Charles Kuhlman, E. A. Lutz, Kristine Lykens, James McDavid, Jerome Milliman, Nancy Neubert, Ronald Oakerson, Elinor Ostrom, Roger Parks, Howard Penniman, Bruce Rogers, Phillip Sabetti, Eric Scott, Dennis Smith, Mark Sproule-Jones, Richard E. Wagner, Murray L. Weidenbaum, York Willbern, Melville Yancey and Donald Zauderer.

Melanie Cloghessy, Rita Murray and Mary Butcher have been most helpful in preparing the final manuscript. Nancy M. Neubert was especially helpful in providing research and editorial assistance at several critical junctures.

The presentation in this monograph has drawn upon an extensive intellectual exchange which we have shared with colleagues in the Center for Urban Affairs at the University of Southern California and in the Workshop in Political Theory and Policy Analysis at Indiana University. Support provided by the Center for the Study of Metropolitan Problems at the National Institute of Mental Health (through grant number 5 R01 MH 19911) to colleagues in the workshop has contributed many essential ingredients to this monograph.

In these circumstances, the costs of public services have also been rising rapidly in major cities, and there is little or no evidence of improvements in service levels accompanying the increasing costs.[1] The eroding quality of urban life and soaring city taxes are accompanied by a substantial measure of citizen alienation. Many citizens feel that they neither receive satisfactory services from city governments nor have much if any say in determining or influencing governmental policies.

When patterns of social relationships generate miserable consequences, reasonable people begin to wonder: What has gone wrong? There is an assumption that social misery, like disease, has its causes. It is further assumed that if the conditions which cause social misery can be understood, a remedy may be available.

It is precisely these assumptions which underlie efforts at governmental reform. Expression of dissatisfaction with the performance of governments in sustaining orderly and productive social relationships and suggestions for improving that performance are so frequent that one is safe to assume that recommendations for reform are as inevitable as death and taxes. Reform is always based upon a diagnosis of some existing conditions that are assumed to produce undesirable results. Reform also depends upon the proposal of some specific course of action which will alter conditions and presumably lead to more desirable outcomes. Such proposals are prescriptions for social change.

Political reform is an effort to modify some aspect in the structure of governmental institutions in order to improve performance. Reform efforts are based upon an assumption that existing governmental structures cause people to order their relationships with one another in a way that is unproductive or dysfunctional. The "rig of the game" leads individuals to pursue opportunities under conditions where people may be left worse off rather than better off. Reform is an effort to change the rules of the game, to modify the rig of the game and to improve the quality of the outcome for everyone concerned. All persons who seek to improve the performance of urban

---

[1] From 1947 to 1967 cost increases of providing a constant level of local services were estimated to be between 5 and 7 percent. Increased expenditure on local government services over the same time period was 9 percent. (D. F. Bradford, R. A. Malt and W. E. Oats, "The Rising Cost of Local Public Services: Some Evidence and Reflections," *National Tax Journal*, vol. 22 [June 1969], pp. 185-202.) Between 1967 and 1970 expenditures of local governments in the largest seventy-two Standard Metropolitan Statistical Areas increased an average of 12 to 13 percent per capita annually. (U.S. Bureau of the Census, *Local Government Finances in Selected Metropolitan Areas and Large Counties: 1970-1971* [Washington, D. C.: U.S. Government Printing Office, 1972], p. 7.)

government by proposing modifications in structural arrangements are participating in reform efforts.

In a recent article on the nature of the "urban crisis," Jerome Zukosky contends that the basic issue in today's crisis may turn upon the use of incorrect diagnoses and improper prescriptions in undertaking efforts at political reform.[2] Under such circumstances we should not be surprised if many governmental reform efforts fail to produce the desired consequences but instead make matters worse. People have long recognized that it is possible for a "remedy" to be worse than a "disease." Perhaps it is time to consider the possibility that the prevailing metropolitan reform orthodoxy has led us to rely upon remedies which are aggravating the situation they are designed to correct. If that is the case, we can expect the urban crisis to deepen—to reach more critical proportions—until we reconsider the causes of what has gone wrong and begin to contemplate different types of remedies.

Zukosky contends that the core problem in the "urban crisis" is a "lack of realistic understanding about how governmental institutions work."[3] More pointedly, the orthodox political science used by traditional metropolitan reformers is lacking in a "realistic understanding" of "how governmental institutions work." Zukosky goes on to conclude that "the urban crisis, therefore, is a crisis of understanding and comprehension, and much broader and more profound a problem than we assume."[4] To deal with this "crisis of understanding" we must know the relationship of reform proposals to basic ideas about how governmental institutions work.[5]

In this brief monograph we shall consider four sets of reform proposals and examine the explanations that are used to justify them. The predominant approach in the metropolitan reform literature of the last century has been to recommend merger and consolidation of the different local governmental units into a single unit of government with general jurisdiction over each metropolitan area. The consolidation approach draws upon a political science that was popularized by Woodrow Wilson and his contemporaries nearly a century ago. A second approach to urban reform has been developed in the

---

[2] Jerome Zukosky, "What's the Problem?" *National Civic Review*, vol. 59 (September 1970), pp. 414-420, 442.

[3] Ibid., p. 414.

[4] Ibid., p. 419.

[5] Vincent Ostrom's *The Intellectual Crisis in American Public Administration* (University, Ala.: University of Alabama Press, 1973) examines the theoretical foundations for both the study and practice of American public administration and the relationship of ideas to action.

last decade by individuals who have called for decentralization, neighborhood governments and community control in order to deal with the unresponsiveness of public service agencies in the nation's larger cities. The proposals advanced by the advocates of community control contradict the conclusions of the consolidationists. Obviously, if consolidation had worked to produce the intended effects, decentralization and community control would not be called for. Simultaneous demands for local community control and for the consolidation of the major units of government in an urban region are also being proposed as a part of a third, "two-tier," approach that combines elements of the first two approaches without reconciling the contradictions in them. These three approaches are examined in Chapter 2.

In addition, a community of scholars who apply the fundamentals of economic reasoning to problems of decision making in the public sector offer still another approach to the organization of urban government. This fourth approach has come to be identified as the public choice approach. This approach is developing a different political science than Wilson and his contemporaries used, a political science akin to the work of Alexander Hamilton, James Madison and Alexis de Tocqueville. The public choice approach is examined in Chapter 3.

We have concluded that the public choice approach provides a more "realistic understanding" about "how governmental institutions work." The relevance of this approach to problems of big city education, crime and police protection, and the provision of fire services is examined in Chapter 4. Issues associated with intergovernmental relations are considered in Chapter 5. In Chapter 6 we review evidence from empirical studies in an effort to determine whether the weight of evidence gives support to our analysis. In the concluding chapter, we give consideration to a number of items which need serious attention on an agenda for the future of urban government.

2
SOME REFORM TRADITIONS

The Old Reform Tradition: Consolidation

From early in the twentieth century until the late 1960s, a single approach to diagnosing problems and prescribing improvements in government has dominated the thinking and recommendations of most analysts of urban government in the United States. That single approach has been called the efficiency and economy reform movement or the good government reform movement.[1]

In 1925 William Anderson succinctly summarized the principal recommendations of this reform tradition:

(1) Each major urban area should be organized by only one unit of local government.

(2) The voters in each major urban area should elect only the most important policy-making officials, and these should be few in number. Citizens will be confused by long ballots and be frustrated in their effort to choose among candidates for numerous public offices.

(3) The traditional separation of powers should be eliminated from the internal structure of the single consolidated unit of local government.

(4) The function of administration, on the other hand, should be separated from that of politics. The work of administration should be performed by specially trained public servants who are adequately compensated, and employed on a full-time basis.

---

[1] For a good summary of the reform tradition for urban governance, see Robert Warren, *Government in Metropolitan Regions: A Reappraisal of Fractionated Political Organization* (Davis: Institute of Governmental Affairs, University of California at Davis, 1966), Chapters 1-3.

(5) Administration should be organized into an integrated command structure in accordance with the hierarchical principle, where authority tapers upward and culminates in a single chief executive.[2]

These principles had also been advanced by Woodrow Wilson during the last decades of the nineteenth century as being essential to good government. Wilson presumed that "the more power is divided the more irresponsible it becomes."[3] He was persuaded that the checks and balances inherent in the American system of government created major impediments to smooth, harmonious relationships in government, and that these checks and balances had "proved mischievous just to the extent to which they had succeeded in establishing themselves as realities."[4]

When considering problems of urban government, analysts in this reform tradition view small units of government as unprofessional and inefficient. The parochial commitment of small jurisdictions to local interests is seen as standing in the way of realizing the overall public interest of the larger metropolitan community. Fragmentation of authority and overlapping jurisdictions among numerous units of local government are diagnosed as the fundamental sources of institutional failure in the government of urban areas.

From this perspective, overlapping jurisdictions imply duplication of services. Duplication of services also implies waste and inefficiency in government. According to these analysts, efficiency is enhanced by eliminating the numerous small jurisdictions and by consolidating all authority in one jurisdiction with general authority to govern each major urban area as a whole. Such consolidations vest ostensibly enlightened leaders and professional administrators with authority to coordinate all aspects of metropolitan affairs through a single integrated structure of government.

Policy analysts in this tradition assume that consolidation of all smaller jurisdictions into a single, overall unit of government for each urban region or metropolitan area clearly fixes political responsibility, making it possible for citizens to hold officials accountable for their actions. Attention to numerous, overlapping jurisdictions presumably overloads citizens, confuses responsibility and frustrates citizens in their efforts to control public policy.

---

[2] William Anderson, *American City Government* (New York: Henry Holt and Company, 1925), pp. 641-642.

[3] Woodrow Wilson, *Congressional Government* (New York: Meridian Books, 1956, originally published in 1885), pp. 77, 187.

[4] Ibid., p. 187.

The persuasiveness of this form of policy analysis is indicated by its use in a major report prepared by the Committee for Economic Development (CED), *Modernizing Local Government*, published in 1966. The CED based its diagnosis upon the following findings:

1. Very few of the local units [of government] are large enough—in population, area or taxable resources—to apply modern methods in solving current and future problems. . . . Even the largest cities find major problems insoluble because of the limits on geographic areas, their taxable resources, or their legal powers.

2. Overlapping layers of local government—municipalities and townships within counties, and independent school districts within them—are a source of weakness. . . . This [overlapping] impairs overall local freedom to deal with vital public affairs; the whole becomes less than the sum of its parts.

3. Popular control over government is ineffective and sporadic, and public interest in local politics is not high. . . . Confusion from the many-layered system, profusion of elective offices without policy significance, and increasing mobility of the population all contribute to disinterest.

4. Policy-making mechanisms in many units are notably weak. The national government [by contrast] has strong executive leadership, supported by competent staff in formulating plans that are then subject to review and modification by a representative legislative body. . . .

5. Antiquated administrative organizations hamper most local governments. Lack of a single executive either elective or appointive is a common fault. Functional fragmentation obscures lines of authority. . . . The quality of administration suffers accordingly.[5]

The reform tradition proposing consolidation of all local governmental units into a single jurisdiction for each metropolitan region has had a powerful appeal. The similarity between textbook ideas and the thoughts of practical men is evident when we compare Anderson's formulation in 1925 with the recommendations made by the CED on how to modernize local government in the 1960s. The CED report included the following recommendations:

1. The number of local governments in the United States, now about 80,000, should be reduced by at least 80 percent.

---

[5] Committee for Economic Development, *Modernizing Local Government* (New York, 1966), pp. 11-12.

[In 1942 William Anderson recommended a reduction in the units of government from 165,000 to 17,800.[6]]

2. The number of overlapping layers of local government found in most states should be severely curtailed.

3. Popular elections should be confined to members of the policy-making body, and to the chief executive in those governments where the "strong mayor" form is preferred to the "council-manager" plan.

4. Each local unit should have a single chief executive, either elected by the people or appointed by the local legislative body, with all administrative agencies and personnel fully responsible to him; election of department heads should be halted.[7]

The theory of government inherent in this reform tradition suggests certain causal relationships among variables. Among these associations are the following: (1) Increasing the size of urban governmental units through consolidation will be associated with improved output of public services, increased efficiency, increased responsibility of local officials and increased confidence among citizens about their capacity to affect public policies. (2) Reducing the multiplicity of jurisdictions serving an urban area through consolidation will also be associated with improved output of public services, increased efficiency, increased responsibility of local officials and increased confidence among citizens about their capacity to affect public policies.

A critical issue in assessing this reform tradition is whether these relationships hold in the operation of urban governments. If these relationships always hold, then the bigger the unit of government and the less duplication the better. If the reverse holds, then the smaller the units of government and the more duplication the better. There may also be intermediate possibilities. For example, an increase in size for some functions might yield improvements to some magnitude and yield net disadvantages beyond that magnitude. In other circumstances a decrease in size might yield improvements to some magnitude but yield net disadvantages if reduced to a still smaller size. These relationships may vary with different types of public goods or services. It is these intermediate possibilities that deserve careful scrutiny.

---

[6] William Anderson, *The Units of Government in the United States: An Enumeration and Analysis* (Chicago: Public Administration Service, 1942), pp. 2, 46.

[7] Committee for Economic Development, *Modernizing Local Government*, p. 17.

The New Reform Movement: Community Control

Since the 1960s there has been a considerable tendency to question the performance of large-scale administrative agencies in the bigger cities of the United States.[8] Citizens' groups have complained about the inability of big city administrative agencies to provide desired police services, perform educational services, get garbage hauled away, resolve traffic problems and carry out other basic functions for which city governments are responsible. These critics do not attribute citizen alienation and rising costs to city government that is too small or to the existence of overlapping jurisdictions, but rather to its largeness, cumbersomeness and monopolistic position. Proponents of community control argue that public bureaucracies in major cities are so large and rigid as to be unmanageable no matter how well intentioned top officials and administrators may be. They also argue that voting for a mayor and few top officials for a large city is insufficient as a means of indicating the variety of citizen preferences.

Citizen preferences, life styles and problems vary from neighborhood to neighborhood. Community control advocates contend that highly centralized governmental units are often unable to respond to these variations among neighborhoods. They have proposed the creation of community councils and quasi-independent neighborhood governments to deal with this problem. They want greater control over government returned to the people so that they will be supplied with the services they prefer rather than an arbitrary level of service that fails to meet their needs. The new reformers have also noted that cost savings do not occur in cities over 100,000 for the most expensive functions such as education and police services, and thus, there is little reason for not organizing some services in relation to neighborhood conditions and assigning control over their provision to community councils or neighborhood governments.

These new reformers demand small enough political units so that (1) the different preferences of different groups of people within urban areas can be more adequately known to public officials, (2) public officials will be located close enough to practical problems so that those officials can be forced to respond to the conditions of life in different neighborhoods, and (3) bureaucracies can be kept small enough so that they are manageable. The demands for community

---

[8] Representative statements of the new reform-community control positions include Milton Kotler, *Neighborhood Government: The Local Foundations of Political Life* (Indianapolis: Bobbs-Merrill, 1969), and Alan A. Altshuler, *Community Control: The Black Demand for Participation in Large American Cities* (New York: Pegasus, 1970).

councils and neighborhood governments within major cities clearly entail a rejection of the basic presumptions inherent in the traditional consolidation approach.

It is not surprising then that proponents of each approach come to rather different conclusions about what is wrong in urban areas and what policies or changes may lead to improvement. The consolidation tradition sees large governmental bureaucracies as directed by enlightened leadership and professional administrators acting efficiently on the basis of a high level of knowledge about their environment. The new reformers see large government bureaucracies as unresponsive, unmanageable, and as lacking knowledge of the multitude of different conditions, neighborhoods, life styles and communities existing in large urban areas. Both are likely to be concerned with rapidly rising costs which exceed general inflationary tendencies. Traditional reformers attribute mushrooming costs to overlapping jurisdictions and duplication of services; the new reformers attribute those cost changes to the bureaucratic inefficiencies in the larger consolidated units of government.

The new reformers demanding community control over the provision of neighborhood public services within large urban areas clearly reject the propositions of the traditional reformers about the relationship of increased size and reduced numbers of jurisdictions to improved services, increased efficiency, increased responsibility of officials and increased confidence among citizens about their capacity to affect public policies. Instead they see increasing consolidation leading to a deterioration in public services, reduced efficiency, decreasing responsibility among officials, and a decreasing confidence among citizens about their capacity to affect public policies.

The Two-Tier Solution

The challenge of the new reformers demanding community control has had a substantial practical appeal, which is reinforced by the observable deterioration of conditions of life in major cities. Officials in the largest cities often contend that urban problems are too great for them to cope with. A crisis exists! And the "crisis" is accompanied by new calls for reform.

One response has been to propose a two-tier solution: consolidation of all *major* units of local government into one general jurisdiction to have authority over all area-wide functions in a metropolitan region together with small local units to deal with community or neighborhood problems within the larger consolidated unit. The two-tier approach has its parallel in the relationship of states with the federal government in a federal system. So the new two-tier approach advances the creation of federated cities.

While differences between the traditional reformers proposing consolidation and the new reformers advocating community control may seem irreconcilable at first glance, there are similarities that have facilitated the formulation of the two-tier solution. These similarities can be noted in a comparison of a recent report by the Committee for Economic Development, *Reshaping Government in Urban Areas,* and a study by Alan Altshuler, *Community Control: The Black Demand for Participation in Large American Cities.* Both were published in 1970.

Between 1966 and 1970 the CED came to recognize that perhaps there was some merit in criticisms of the unresponsiveness of large city bureaucracies. The new report indicates a willingness to sacrifice "neatness and symmetry" for greater "effectiveness and responsiveness."[9] It recommends a two-tier arrangement for the reform of government in metropolitan areas. The top tier would be an all inclusive area-wide metropolitan government, but it would be supplemented by a bottom tier of small governments throughout each metropolitan area to better assist neighborhoods to articulate their different preferences and permit the provision of some public goods and services by smaller and more responsive units.

In his study, Altshuler points out that advocates of community control could easily agree with reformers on the abolition of special districts and on simplification of the internal government structure (a single council of a few elected officials and a single strong executive) of any particular unit of government. Supporters of community control would not oppose the creation of a metropolitan area-wide government, so long as a second tier of smaller governments is created with authority to provide those services of most concern to local communities and neighborhoods.[10] Thus, on the question of future reform in patterns of urban government, the traditional reformers advocating consolidation and the new reformers advocating community control may find common ground in the two-tier approach.

Altshuler and the 1970 CED position both represent pragmatic compromises without explicit exploration of the implications of the factors which permit the compromise solution to emerge. One important factor facilitating the compromise is joint recognition of the differences in the nature of many public goods and services. The

---

[9] Committee for Economic Development, *Reshaping Urban Government* (New York, 1970), p. 19.
[10] Altshuler, *Community Control,* pp. 50-51.

most enthusiastic advocates of community control recognize that there is a role for larger governmental units to control air pollution, provide large regional water supply and sewer systems, create mass transportation facilities and redistribute income to improve the fiscal capabilities of lower income communities. There is less agreement on which specific functions are appropriate subjects for local community control. It also appears that traditional reformers are modifying their position with a recognition that different groups of people may prefer different mixes and levels of public goods and services and that bureaucracies organized on an area-wide basis for all public functions may not be the most efficient way to respond to the diversities within each metropolitan area.

The recognition that different citizens can legitimately have different preferences and tastes for public goods and services and wish to enjoy different life styles represents a major change from earlier reform arguments that a uniform level of public services, as decided upon by officials representing the community as a whole, should be provided to everyone. The recognition of a diversity in preferences is a major premise of the new reformers advocating community control. A compromise on this point by traditional reformers advocating consolidation is essential to agreement upon a two-tier structure of governments for metropolitan areas.

The compromise afforded by the two-tier solution, however, glosses over the basic challenge to the traditional reform movement made by the advocates of community control. The challenge implies that the logic inherent in the consolidation solution did not stand the test of experience. Where successful consolidation movements have created overall units of city government, as in the cases of New York (1898), Philadelphia (1854) and St. Louis (1875) among many others, the logic of consolidation failed to cope with the problem of providing the means to deal with neighborhood problems. In fact, even the essentially two-tier structure of the New York City borough system has not been sufficient to deal with neighborhood problems.[11]

Academic discussion about a single unit of metropolitan government performing area-wide functions appears most reasonable until one confronts the practical problem of specifying boundaries for

---

[11] It is interesting to note that the two-tier structure in New York City has been the subject of reform efforts directed at moving toward greater centralization by reducing the power and functions of boroughs and increasing the power of the city. Such reforms were undertaken as recently as the early 1960s. In the 1970s, demands for decentralization and community control have focused upon areas of much smaller size than the existing boroughs.

metropolitan regions. Just how inclusive is the overall tier to be? Are Washington and Baltimore, Philadelphia, Camden and Trenton, Newark and New York, and New Haven, Providence and Boston to be grouped in several urban regions or in a single region? In confronting the practical problem of drawing boundaries for the urban agglomerations of the Atlantic Seaboard, the Great Lakes, California or the Puget-Willamette Trough of the Pacific Northwest, the difficulties of devising a single unit of government capable of dealing with area-wide problems become overwhelming.

On the other hand, what size government is appropriate to deal with community problems as the lower tier of a federated urban government? The communities of interest and the scope of problems vary in size, and a single lower tier of governments for a large megalopolis may be insufficient to deal with them appropriately. What criteria can be applied to the design of a two-tier structure? The practical man may very well ask: Do we have any reason to believe that a two-tier approach will be sufficient to provide solutions to the range of problems confronting people in any major urban agglomeration?

Conclusion

The demands for community control have presented a basic challenge to the logic of consolidation. That challenge created what Jerome Zukosky has called "a crisis of understanding."[12] The logic of consolidation has not provided a "realistic understanding about how governmental institutions work." Large consolidated city governments have experienced the worst of the urban crisis. We must turn elsewhere to develop a more realistic understanding about how governmental institutions work.

A recognition that different public goods and services possess different characteristics and that individuals may have different tastes for public goods and services provided the basis for a pragmatic two-tier compromise between advocates of consolidation and the new reformers espousing community control. The same conditions—a recognition that public goods and services come in different shapes and sizes and that individuals have different life styles associated with tastes for the provision of different public goods and services— provides the basis for another approach to understanding how urban government works. That approach is the subject of the next chapter.

---

[12] Zukosky, "What's the Problem?" *National Civic Review*, vol. 59 (September 1970).

3

THE PUBLIC CHOICE APPROACH

Introduction

The diagnoses and prescriptions of traditional reformers and the new advocates of community control constitute two major approaches to problems of urban government. An alternative way of thinking takes as its starting point the diversity of individual preferences and the diverse nature of goods and services rather than organization structure. This alternative approach is usually called the political economy or public choice approach. It has a long history, although it has often been obscured in the twentieth century. The best statements and examples of this way of thinking are contained in the essays by Alexander Hamilton and James Madison in *The Federalist*, Alexis de Tocqueville's *Democracy in America* and the contemporary writing of public choice economists and political scientists such as James Buchanan, Gordon Tullock, Charles Lindblom and Mancur Olson.[1]

---

[1] For an analysis of how the authors of *The Federalist* approached political analysis, see Vincent Ostrom, *The Political Theory of a Compound Republic: A Reconstruction of the Logical Foundations of American Democracy as Presented in "The Federalist"* (Blacksburg, Virginia: Virginia Polytechnic Institute, Center for the Study of Public Choice, 1971). The most explicit application of public choice theory to the analysis of urban governance is contained in Vincent Ostrom, Charles Tiebout, and Robert Warren, "The Organization of Government in Metropolitan Areas," *American Political Science Review*, vol. 55 (December 1961), pp. 831-842, and Robert L. Bish, *The Public Economy of Metropolitan Areas* (Chicago: Markham, 1971). Other major writings utilizing a public choice approach include James M. Buchanan and Gordon Tullock, *The Calculus of Consent* (Ann Arbor: University of Michigan Press, 1962); Mancur Olson, *The Logic of Collective Action* (Cambridge: Harvard University Press, 1965), Gordon Tullock, *The Politics of Bureaucracy* (Washington, D. C.: Public Affairs Press, 1965); Charles Lindblom, *The Intelligence of Democracy* (New York: The Free Press, 1965). For a discussion of the development of the public choice approach and several hundred additional references see Vincent Ostrom and

Assumptions about individuals. The public choice approach to the analysis of urban problems begins with a focus on individuals. Individuals are assumed to act on a knowledge of the alternatives that may be available to them. Such knowledge is assumed to be imperfect. As a consequence, individuals are expected to be fallible, and individuals will find information costly to acquire.[2] The conditions of fallibility and costliness of information applies to all decision makers, citizens, officials, professional experts, public employees, et cetera.

Individuals are also assumed to have diverse preferences and to weigh alternative possibilities in relation to their preferences. Individuals will choose those possibilities that they believe will gain them the greatest net advantage. All individuals are seen as self-interested, but self-interest may include a personal concern for the welfare of others.

Individuals are also assumed to exist in a society in which decision rules are used as a means for ordering relationships among individuals and in which some individuals occupying specialized positions are assigned governmental prerogatives to determine, enforce and alter legal relationships. For purposes of this analysis, we shall assume the existence of a constitutional order under which rules applicable to the conduct of government can be enforced against those who exercise governmental prerogatives at all levels of government. Thus, the exercise of local government authority contrary to the basic criteria of constitutional law and legislation consistent with constitutional authority is assumed to be unlawful. Persons are assumed correlatively to have access to judicial, legislative and constitutional remedies in seeking redress against officials and governments which violate constitutional rights or rights created under legislative authority of the state and federal governments. Relevant standards of state and national laws are assumed to be enforceable in relation to the conduct of local officials and local governments.

Assumptions about goods and services. Among the array of possibilities, individual citizens are assumed to have their own preferences for both public and private goods. The goods themselves possess diverse characteristics. Some, such as apples or bread, can be dealt

---

Elinor Ostrom, "Public Choice: A Different Approach to the Study of Public Administration," *Public Administration Review*, vol. 31 (March/April 1971), pp. 203-216.

[2] For analyses of information problems see F. A. Hayek, "The Uses of Knowledge in Society," *American Economic Review*, vol. 35 (September 1945), pp. 519-530, and Gordon Tullock, *The Politics of Bureaucracy*.

with efficiently under private market arrangements, with public action required only to assure free market conditions, to maintain enforceability of contracts and to resolve disputes between individuals participating in market transactions. Private goods, like apples and bread, are highly divisible and packageable. Individuals can be excluded from consuming them unless they are willing to pay the price. Markets work reasonably well for most packageable goods where potential buyers can be excluded from the use of a good unless they are willing to pay the price to acquire it.

Other goods and services, such as national defense, police services, fire protection, control of contagious diseases, quality of the environment and income redistribution, are thought not to be susceptible to adequate handling in private markets. Men have formed governments to assist with the provision of these goods.

Public goods and services share the characteristic of being enjoyed or consumed by all members of a community in common. Individuals *cannot be excluded* from enjoying a public good once it is provided for someone else; and one individual's consumption or enjoyment will not subtract from its consumption or enjoyment by others. For example, once peace and security are provided in a community, they are available for anyone to enjoy. My enjoyment of that peace and security does not subtract from others enjoying that same peace and security. Yet peace and security do not just happen. They depend upon the organized activities of many people and require the expenditure of substantial time and effort.

Assumptions about organizations. Public goods and services probably cannot be provided on a stable, long-term basis through purely voluntary efforts and financing. If payments were purely voluntary, each citizen would find it in his own interest to withhold payment so long as enough others paid to keep the benefits flowing. The result of many individuals withholding payment would be inadequate provision of public goods and services. Resolution of this dilemma is usually sought through some form of governmental organization. In this respect, government serves as a coercive means of seeing to it that each individual contributes his share, through the payment of taxes, for the provision of public goods and services.[3]

Governmental organizations also provide means for citizens to communicate their preferences for public goods and services through such mechanisms as elections. The provision of public goods and services by governmental agencies is evaluated by reference to

---

[3] The logic of this issue is treated in Bish, *Public Economy*, Chapters 2 and 3.

citizen preferences. From this perspective, government is not an end in itself but a means to provide for goods and services which are enjoyed in common by communities of individuals. Merely providing public goods and services without reference to citizen preferences makes no economic sense. Thus, the major question when diagnosing the performance of governments is how efficiently they provide citizens with the public goods and services that citizens prefer.

Different forms or structures of governmental organization create different incentives for public officials and public employees to "serve" the preferences of citizens or to ignore their preferences. The incentives created by different forms of organization will thus affect the efficiency with which producers of public goods and services respond to the preferences of citizens. This focus is different from that of the traditional reform movement—in which the focus is on strengthening the authority of knowledgeable, benevolent leaders to determine all subordinate interests.

The public choice approach, however, is often congruent with the analysis made by the advocates of community control who also recognize the diversity of citizen preferences for different public goods and services. The public choice approach is more inclusive than that of the community control approach since it provides criteria for determining which goods are most appropriately provided on a national or regional basis as well as which goods are best provided by relatively small political units.

When a good or service is used in common it is often possible to specify boundaries which encompass the community of people affected by the provision of that public good or service. A ground water basin, for example, may have quite precise boundaries, and the creation of a ground water replenishment district would need to take account of those who benefit from its use. An "air-shed" has less precise boundaries, but an air pollution control program would need to take account of the community of interests existing among polluters and users of the particular atmospheric conditions which might be thought of as an air-shed.

Some uses of roads, streets and highways, on the other hand, may be highly localized and the relevant community may be confined to a small enclave. Other streets may be principal thoroughfares that are used by a much larger community of people. Still other highways may be used principally by interstate and national communities of users. If each different community is to be able to make optimal use of an interconnected system of neighborhood streets, urban thoroughfares and interstate highways, then different communities need

20

to be organized. Their diverse preferences are taken into account only when the different communities participate in decisions about the uses which are of interest to them.[4]

We would expect the patterns of organization to influence the way that streets and highways are designed and used. In St. Louis, Missouri, for example, purely residential streets are sometimes organized as "private" streets where neighborhood associations assume responsibility for regulating their use and providing for their maintenance. Neighborhood interests are allowed to dominate, and those streets can be used by children on bicycles or rollerskates with minimal danger from automobiles. Without an appropriate organizational arrangement for neighbors to assume responsibility for neighborhood streets, every street is apt to become a thoroughfare dominated by automobile traffic as drivers seek out neighborhood streets to avoid other more congested thoroughfares. Without larger jurisdictions to provide major thoroughfares, however, local neighborhood associations would probably seek to avoid the problems of through traffic by diverting it elsewhere. Thus, both large and small jurisdictions of varying size seem to be necessary for the development, maintenance and use of a network of streets, thoroughfares and highways which serve diverse communities of interest.

Criteria for evaluating performance. The performance of governments, in the public choice approach, should be evaluated in terms of criteria which can be applied by citizens as well as officials. Criteria such as efficiency, responsiveness, and fairness or equity should apply to the performance of governments as well as to other activities.

The minimal condition for efficiency, for example, is that benefits exceed costs. The comparative efficiency of different organizations can be determined by which one provides the greatest surplus of benefits over costs. Because of measurement and budgetary problems in public sector activities, we may have to be content with determining which alternative provides a given level of service at least cost, or equivalently, which provides the best service for a given level of expenditure. Difficulties in finding appropriate measures of output usually require that proxy measures be used as indicators of output. A least-cost solution may then become a measure of producer efficiency in the absence of a measure of user or consumer satisfaction.

Difficulties in determining consumer satisfaction or demand in the absence of competitive pricing arrangements mean that respon-

---

[4] Robert Kanigel, "Improving City Streets to Death," *City*, vol. 6 (Winter 1972), pp. 45-47.

siveness must also be taken into account in evaluating the performance of governmental agencies. Responsiveness can be defined as the capacity of a governmental organization to satisfy the preferences of citizens. The criterion of responsiveness is based upon the premise that individuals are the best judges of their own interests. Measures of responsiveness usually depend upon interviews conducted in a sample survey of a relevant population of citizens.

In the final analysis, benefits can be calculated only in relation to user preferences, and the criteria of efficiency and responsiveness are interdependent. The criteria of efficiency must include responsiveness as an essential component. However, the difficulty of measuring and evaluating public goods and services requires us to take account of both efficiency and responsiveness as separate but related criteria in evaluating the performance of public agencies.

The criterion of fairness or equity is difficult to formulate in a way that can be used to measure comparative performance. Still other criteria bearing upon organizational tendencies to amplify or correct errors might also be used. Our discussions will focus primarily upon efficiency and responsiveness as criteria for evaluating performance.

In this brief summary of the public choice approach we have made certain assumptions about individuals. We have also indicated what we consider the essential difference between private and public goods and services and why we believe that market organization and voluntary arrangements will fail to provide a satisfactory level of public goods and services. We have also set forth our conclusion that some form of governmental organization is a necessary condition for overcoming the hold-out problem which can plague voluntary efforts to provide public goods and services. And we have indicated criteria that can be used to assess performance. In the sections which follow, we shall consider some of the difficulties in dealing with demand and supply in the public sector. From this analysis we should be able to reach some preliminary conclusions about what structural arrangements for the organization of government in metropolitan areas will enhance responsiveness and efficiency.

Demand

In the private sector, preferences are indicated when consumers shop around to purchase products from different suppliers. Willingness to pay the price is an indication of consumer preference. Exchanges of this type seldom occur in the public sector. Instead, preferences for public goods and services are expressed through voting, lobbying, public opinion polls, petitions, public hearings, demonstrations, court proceedings, political party organizations and other indirect manners, including recourse to violence and civil disobedience when things are desperate. None of these institutional arrangements translate preferences into products in a perfectly responsive manner. What is more, incentive systems within such arrangements frequently lead citizens to "demand" public goods, not because they value the goods more than the cost of producing the goods but because taxing mechanisms disassociate costs from benefits and in some cases—perhaps many— put the costs on somebody else.

It is difficult, if not impossible, to identify "true" citizen preferences or demands for public goods. The incentives created by structures of institutional arrangements will affect the way that preferences are expressed in much the same way that light affects what we see. We can never see the "true" nature of reality. But we can become aware of how different spectacles and filters will affect our vision. We can also discover how different institutional mechanisms affect expressions of preferences.

Voting, either directly on issues or for representatives who in turn vote on issues, is one of the major ways in which demands for public goods and services are expressed.[5] Voting has several weaknesses as compared to market exchanges, however. A single vote usually has to serve as an expression of preference on many issues simultaneously, and it may not represent the voter's preferences on all the issues at hand. For example, a single vote for President entails "endorsement" of a candidate's positions on issues ranging from expansion of trade with China to the introduction of a negative income tax. Most often, however, a voter does not agree with a candidate on all issues, and thus, the vote he casts does not reflect all of his preferences.

Even in single-issue voting, such as for school bonds, voters are limited to an all-or-nothing choice. No opportunity exists to select desired amounts. These problems of voting are sometimes referred to as the "all-or-nothing blue-plate menu problem," where à la carte purchasing is not permitted.

The problem of having only a single vote to express preferences on a wide variety of issues is diminished as governmental units become more numerous and specialized in their range of functions.

---

[5] Good analyses of voting problems are contained in James Buchanan, "Individual Choice in Voting and the Market," in *Fiscal Theory and Political Economy* (Chapel Hill: University of North Carolina Press, 1960), and in Anthony Downs, *An Economic Theory of Democracy* (New York: Harper and Row, 1958).

Of course, the physical supply characteristics of many public goods may restrict the minimum size of an appropriate political unit. An air pollution control district, for example, with jurisdiction over an entire air-shed will be better able to provide the service of air pollution control. In addition, relations among some services may make it efficient to group them together—such as placing elementary and secondary education under the same school board. The specific organization of the public sector—which and what size political units are responsible for which public goods and services—can make considerable difference in a citizen's ability to voice his preferences accurately through the voting process.

Voting is not the only way in which citizens indicate their preferences to political officials. The opportunities to lobby, go to court, write letters or speak to officials, file petitions, testify at hearings or express feelings on individual issues in public opinion polls, all provide citizens with ways of expressing preferences more precisely on single issues. However, while preferences may be expressed more precisely, different citizens will have different opportunities for access. Further, given the costs of participation, citizens will not be motivated to indicate their preferences unless they feel that the benefits of such activity will exceed the costs.[6] Consequently, stronger incentives exist for citizens to express preferences for special programs of direct and measurable benefit to themselves than for policies which may provide small benefits to large numbers of citizens over a wide area.

Citizen demands can be more precisely indicated in smaller rather than larger political units, and in political units undertaking fewer rather than more numerous public functions. This potential advantage must be compared with the costs of indicating preferences to many different political units. Citizens will be unlikely to find complete preference articulation easier with a single small unit for each public service. The optimal situation is more likely to be one in which each of several units performs multiple services.

Another factor which can affect the relative sensitivity or insensitivity of a political system in responding to citizen preferences is the effect of size upon patterns of leadership recruitment and political entrepreneurship. The costs of becoming a candidate for public office with a reasonable probability of success are low in a small town where an individual is well known by his neighbors and fellow towns-

---

[6] Mark Sproule-Jones and Kenneth D. Hart, "A Public Choice Model of Political Participation," *Canadian Journal of Political Science*, vol. 6, forthcoming 1973: and Mark Sproule-Jones, "Citizen Participation in a Canadian Municipality," *Public Choice*, vol. 16, forthcoming 1974.

men. The cost of becoming a candidate for President of the United States is of radically larger proportions. Individuals in small jurisdictions may find it relatively easy to aspire to positions of local leadership.

Moisei Ostrogorski in his study, *Democracy and the Organization of Political Parties*, recognized that American cities with populations in excess of 100,000 appear to be subject to a basic shift in patterns of leadership recruitment and political entrepreneurship.[7] Costs of political campaigning increase to a point where some individuals have an incentive to develop a political organization and offer a whole slate of candidates for public office. An individual has much less probability of success unless he is slated by the organization and can gain the advantage of its resources. An organization, in this sense, may be a political party or a "nonpartisan" civic group.

The organization in turn is confronted with a problem of covering its costs of operation. If it is successful in electing its slate, the organization can take advantage of opportunities for public employment and its control over governmental decisions to reward its supporters and put together the combination of resources necessary for its continued success.

So long as active political rivalry exists among competing organizations, professional politicians as political entrepreneurs will still be constrained by the necessity of appealing to a majority of the electorate. Citizen preferences will have a significant influence upon public policies. However, if any one entrepreneur becomes sufficiently dominant, he can use the police and other government organs to collect payoffs to finance the organization, and his men can coerce voters to turn out and vote for the organization slate. Such entrepreneurs can operate as political bosses, with "civic leaders" becoming their obedient servants. Ostrogorski considered such patterns of organization to be a function of size and he suggested that bossism would be more prevalent in large cities than in smaller cities.[8]

Opportunities for political entrepreneurship will also be significantly affected by types of elections, forms of ballots and modes of representation as well as size of jurisdiction. However, the conditions favored by reformers proposing consolidation—short ballots and at-large elections—would appear to be those which are most conducive to the success of professional politicians seeking to preempt

---

[7] Moisei Ostrogorski, *Democracy and the Organization of Political Parties: The United States*, vol. 2 (Garden City, N. Y.: Doubleday and Co., Anchor Books, 1964). See generally his discussion in Part V.

[8] Ibid., pp. 213-214.

leadership recruitment through a permanent organization for slating candidates and canvassing voters. Advocates of consolidation do not necessarily object to such patterns of political organization, but are concerned that the organization winning control of the government be "responsible" to the electorate. How that might be done in the absence of benevolent organization men remains an unanswered problem.

Expression of demand in public organizations is plagued with persistent difficulties. Large organizations, in the sense that they encompass large populations and territory, can respond in relation to those problems which are uniformly experienced by everyone within their reach. The quality of the atmosphere and the conditions of major transportation networks, for example, have widespread and similar effects upon large numbers of people. Where neighborhood conditions and people's preferences vary substantially from one sub-area to another, however, information about these variations is apt to be lost if people have recourse only to a single large unit of government. Both large and small units of government appear to be necessary if people are to be able to express their demands for different types of public goods and services.

Supply

In addition to the expression of preference, supply and management considerations must be taken into account when analyzing the organization of public service agencies in metropolitan areas. As with preference articulation, the nature of public goods and services also creates difficulties on the supply side that are not encountered by a private firm producing a private good or service.[9]

First, it is very difficult to measure, let alone evaluate, most public services. For example, how does one effectively measure and value all the different outputs of a court system, a police system or an educational system? Not only are outputs difficult to measure and assign values but the same production inputs will result in different outputs depending on the characteristics of the area served. For example, sewers will require relatively more expenditures of resources to provide a given level of sanitation in hilly, low density areas, while fire services will require relatively more resources to provide a given

---

[9] A good survey of supply problems is contained in Werner Hirsch, "The Supply of Urban Government Services," in Harvey S. Perloff and Lowden Wingo, Jr., eds. *Issues in Urban Economics* (Baltimore: The Johns Hopkins Press, 1968).

level of protection in high density areas containing many adjacent multi-story buildings. In addition, the same production process may provide different benefits and be valued differently by individuals with different opportunities to use the services provided. For example, we would expect students from Spanish-speaking homes to find it more difficult to benefit from the educational services provided in most schools than students from English-speaking homes.

Public services which are capital intensive in the sense that a large proportion of the cost involved is tied up in physical plant and public works are the most amenable to large-scale organization. Transportation facilities, water supply systems and sewerage works are examples of capital intensive services. These types of services usually emphasize physical effects, are more amenable to measurement and require proportionately smaller numbers of permanent employees in relation to the population served.

Many other public goods and services are highly labor intensive in their production. Payments to labor often account for 80 to 95 percent of the cost of a public service. The lack of physical output measurements in labor intensive services makes it extremely difficult to determine an employee's contribution to an organization's production, and the service nature of the public function makes the value of the output highly dependent on the quality of individual employee-citizen relationships. For example, patrolman-citizen relationships strongly affect citizen evaluation of police services and teacher-student relationships strongly affect citizen evaluation of educational services.

The administrator at the top of an organizational hierarchy simply has no easy check on the adequacy with which his subordinates discharge their public services in person-to-person relationships. He faces a real dilemma in how to direct his organization. The greater the uniformity of production processes, rules and quality of particular service activities, the easier it will be to monitor and control a large organization. However, the more uniform the output, the less likely that those citizens whose preferences and problems differ from the average will be satisfied with the service product. One must keep in mind that it is not the producers *as people* in public organizations that create the difficulty. The goods and services provided are not easily measurable and packageable. Thus public goods and services do not lend themselves to being produced by a firm that can rely heavily on measurements of sales compared with costs to determine efficiency.

The difficulty in measuring and evaluating the output of public service agencies leads to profound problems in organizing the public sector. Without an effective indicator of output it becomes difficult, if not impossible, to determine when the costs of production exceed the value of the service rendered. Top administrators depend upon management controls to direct the actions of employees who render a public service. However, there is no automatic way to determine when increased management costs associated with increases in organizational size exceed the benefit to be derived from adding extra employees.

These tendencies are exaggerated by the circumstance in which greater political prestige is associated with heading a large organization rather than a small organization. In addition, the greater number of steps in a career ladder for a large organization involve greater opportunities for advancement, and the most desirable positions in terms of high salaries and other perquisites are usually associated with management activities rather than service opportunities. Large expenditures for management create the most attractive career opportunities in most public organizations. All of these opportunities exist without reference to incentives for either improving the quality of public services or the net efficiency of public agencies. Public agencies with access to large fiscal resources have few if any incentives to economize.

The problems of measurement and evaluation of outputs necessary to determine production efficiency are not entirely unique to the public sector. For example, many of the service industries, such as advertising, interior decoration and law and medical practice, often face similar difficulties. However, in the private sector, failure to provide services comparable to those obtainable from competitors leads to a decline in business—and a very clear indication to the producer that something is wrong. Furthermore, if adaptability to meet competition is not achieved, inefficient producers are forced to accept less pay or move into some other area of economic activity. Competition among producers is much less present in the public sector.

In the economic analysis of private monopolies it is usually assumed that the monopoly firm will attempt to maximize profits although the quantity produced is less than would be produced by competitive firms. No simple assumption such as profit maximization is suitable for beginning an analysis of public agencies because the output is not generally priced and sold, and if it were, public officials probably would not be allowed to capture the profits for themselves.

A government is often conceived of as a natural monopoly which exercises exclusive control over the supply of a good or service in a given market area. A unit of government can occupy a monopoly position when that unit is the exclusive supplier of a good or service for local residents. Problems associated with monopoly organization have substantial implications for governmental performance.

Government organizations operating under monopoly conditions will have little incentive to innovate or reduce costs. Few employees will have an incentive to rock the boat because the costs of innovation will be relatively high in proportion to the benefit that the individual can derive. Most administrators and employees may prefer to settle into leisurely routines rather than fight the system in attempts to modify operations to meet citizen preferences. Small monopolies can be as lethargic as big monopolies. Needless to say, such behavior is not likely to lead to outputs efficiently produced to meet citizen preferences. The monopoly position of the public producer may protect him from individual citizens, even if he is inefficient and unresponsive in meeting their demands.[10]

Public monopolies pose even more difficult problems than private monopolies. With private monopolies we can assume that consumers will obtain net benefits from their purchases. Problems of unresponsive monopolistic behavior where outputs are not easily measured or evaluated and where political power can be used by a public monopolist to collect taxes for maintaining his organization are potentially more serious than problems of private monopolistic behavior. Public monopolists without an appropriate structure of incentives can be even less responsive and less efficient than private monopolists.

The essential question regarding the organization of governments in metropolitan areas is this: Would we expect a fully integrated unit of government occupying a monopoly position over the production of all public goods and services to produce all goods and services equally well? On the basis of our analysis we have reason to believe that the answer is "no." We would not expect a fully integrated monopoly created by the consolidation of all public organizations in a metropolitan area to be equally effective in operating large-scale systems of physical works and in performing a variety of highly personalized public services in which person-to-person relationships critically affect the quality of service.

---

[10] Robert L. Bish and Robert Warren, "Scale and Monopoly Problems in Urban Government Services," *Urban Affairs Quarterly*, vol. 8 (September 1972), pp. 97-122.

Instead we assume that the diverse nature of events in the world and the diverse preferences and life styles of people will make having recourse to multiple jurisdictions, both large and small, advantageous in the organization of urban governments. Rivalry and competition can alleviate some of the most adverse consequences of monopoly behavior in the public sector. If ample fragmentation of authority and overlapping jurisdictions exist, sufficient competition may be engendered to stimulate a more responsive and efficient public economy in metropolitan areas.

There are several ways that competition can constrain the monopolistic behavior of public officials. One is political competition, contests for elective office. If responsiveness and efficiency of the government drop below citizens' expectations, they can vote the incumbents out in the hope that their opponents will improve the government's outputs. However, in large central cities, such as New York, it is not clear that even the most highly motivated elected officials can effectively manage the various agencies of government subject to their authority. The large number of employees and the difficulty of measuring outputs are simply too great.

A second kind of competition can occur when people "vote with their feet." [11] If a citizen is dissatisfied with the benefits received from the local government where he resides he can simply move to a governmental unit where the level and mix of services relative to the tax payments comes closer to meeting his preferences. Most metropolitan areas contain many different local government jurisdictions. Suburbanization in metropolitan areas may well reflect citizen dissatisfaction with the high costs and poor services rendered in central cities. If a person feels that good schools are important for his children and he cannot afford the tuition of private schools, the solution may be to move to a suburban school district where his family can secure the education he wants for it.

Still another kind of competition can occur when individuals seek out alternative producers of public goods without changing location. For example, firms, shopping centers and residents in wealthy neighborhoods often hire private police to patrol their areas when public police protection is considered inadequate. Private schools also offer an alternative to the public school system. Options may also be available for urban citizens to seek goods or services from overlapping governments instead of relying exclusively upon

---

[11] The first explicit analysis of voting with one's feet to obtain preferred public goods is contained in Charles M. Tiebout, "A Pure Theory of Local Expenditures," *Journal of Political Economy*, vol. 64 (October 1956), pp. 416-424.

their city for services normally provided by a city. City police corruption may lead citizens, for example, to seek recourse to the county sheriffs or to state police. An important feature of the American federal system is overlapping levels of government, making it possible for a citizen unhappy with the services at one level to seek recourse at another.

Competition can also occur among different public agencies if ample overlap exists. One unit of government may operate as a buyers' cooperative on behalf of local residents and firms rather than becoming a monopoly producer itself. In that case the local jurisdiction would have the power to tax and to use tax funds to arrange for some other agency to produce a public good or service. Such producers might be private enterprises as well as public agencies. So long as alternative producers are available, a local jurisdiction operating as a buyers' cooperative can press for the best deal. In such a situation producers will have incentives to improve the quality of services, increase efficiency and introduce viable innovations. The jurisdiction buying services might contract with a private vendor for street sweeping, with a public agency for police services and so on, thus using an array of different vendors to serve the community. Its chief administrative officer would operate as a purchasing agent demanding performance from vendors. Contracting for public goods provision permits smaller jurisdictions, which can best express the demands of local residents for varying mixes of public goods and services, to achieve efficient operation by purchasing their public goods from other agencies—private and public—which are the most efficient producers of those public goods and services.

Local governments in a democratic federal system of government are not pure monopolists. Citizens do have alternatives available to them which can generate competition. Competitive pressures can occur when people seek recourse by electing different officials, voting with their feet, using private alternatives or through other levels of government. However, all of these options have costs, and many of these costs may be hard for low income and minority citizens to pay. The cost of voting with their feet, for example, may be too great for many poor people. The cost of making their demands known to city hall may also be too high for them to pay. They may have little option but to bear the burden of poverty until alternative structures can be devised both to facilitate a redistribution of income and to provide governmental units that are more responsive to the demands of the poor. The poor are most in need of neighborhood governments in which the costs of articulating demands can be kept to a minimum.

Conclusion

Even this brief analysis of the expression of demand, production and management problems in the public sector indicates that the task of organizing an efficient and responsive set of public services to serve the diverse needs of citizens in urban areas is not an easy one. The problems are such that private markets cannot be relied upon for many needs. As soon as governments are created to provide public goods and services, officials find it difficult to identify citizen demands accurately. Officials may also simply ignore citizen demands and act like monopolists. Neither private markets nor political organizations produce perfect solutions, but raising questions within this framework offers an alternative way of thinking about the design of political structures for the government of urban areas. When diverse preferences for different public goods are recognized to exist, there are few simple answers to problems of governmental organization.

Before moving on to apply the public choice approach to the organization of educational services, police services, fire services and intergovernmental relations, it will be useful to summarize a few key issues that public choice analysts treat in their studies of political organization:

(1) Nature of the good. Does production and consumption occur simultaneously in interpersonal relationships (like education and police patrol), or is it a physical product like water or sewers? The more face-to-face contact that is required, the more difficult it will be to manage a large organization because of the difficulties in controlling the quality of interpersonal relationships and of measuring outputs.

(2) Scale of production effects. What geographic area is covered by the field of effects which are enjoyed or used in common? Air pollution control must cover an entire air-shed, but elementary education can be provided in a small neighborhood.

(3) Demand articulation. Can all citizens articulate their preferences? How many issues are included in a single voting process? How much voice does the individual citizen have in public decisions?

(4) Professionalization. Professionalization within organizations enhances reliability and predictability. Does it also encourage the substitution of professional judgments for citizen preferences?

(5) Choice. What recourse do citizens have if they are dissatisfied with the outputs of a single political unit? Are there over-

lapping units to provide some alternatives? How far would citizens have to move to find a more satisfactory arrangement? How costly are private alternatives?

(6) Competition. Do opportunities exist among the various jurisdictions in a metropolitan area to contract for public services? Do the smaller jurisdictions behave like buyers' cooperatives working on behalf of local residents and firms? Are private vendors as well as public agencies contracted with? Do the different agencies take advantage of each other's diverse capabilities?

(7) Innovation. Are there incentives for government employees to improve efficiency, or do incentives encourage maintenance of routine operations with little exposure to competitive rivalry?

Many of the issues raised in the public choice approach are also raised by advocates of community control. Public choice analysts would not expect single, area-wide metropolitan governments to perform equally well in meeting citizen preferences efficiently for *all* public goods and services. A two-tier arrangement would enhance efficiency and responsiveness. But two-tier arrangements for the large urban regions characteristic of the Atlantic Seaboard and Southern California would probably be insufficient to deal with the diverse demand and supply schedules for all public goods and services over such large areas.

One can only go so far in analyzing the performance of governments in urban areas by abstract concepts. Whether one or another concept is more helpful in the design of institutions for urban government will depend upon the evidence about how well governmental institutions perform under varying conditions. In the following two chapters, issues and empirical evidence surrounding problems of organization in the provision of education, police services, fire protection and intergovernmental relationships will be presented. Following this presentation, we will return to the question of which approach stands up best to comparisons with empirical evidence.

4
EDUCATION, POLICE SERVICES AND FIRE PROTECTION

Many public functions could be selected for examination in a discussion of urban government. The three functions considered here have been selected because of their importance and because empirical evidence can be used to clarify the issues raised in previous chapters.

Big City Education

Big city school systems are commonly recognized to be in trouble, trouble relating to poor performance by students, high dropout rates, alienation of students and parents and rising costs.[1] In New York City, for example, student scores on reading proficiency are continuing to decline, and educators there and "in most big cities have been unable to find ways to reverse this trend."[2] Over 50 percent of the black and Puerto Rican students drop out before graduation from high school.[3] In Bedford-Stuyvesant, an area of 450,000 people within New York City served by *one* high school, over 80 percent of the students drop out prior to high school graduation.[4]

Dissatisfaction with big city schools is not confined to low-income or racial minorities. In Boston higher income residents send only 62.3 percent of their children to public elementary school, in

---

[1] Recent analysis of big city school systems include: Marilyn Gittell, ed. *Educating an Urban Population* (Beverly Hills, Calif.: Sage Publications, 1967), and Marilyn Gittell et al., *School Decentralization and School Policy in New York City* (A Report for the New York State Commission on the Quality, Cost and Financing of Elementary and Secondary Education, 1971).

[2] *New York Times*, May 27, 1973, p. 1.

[3] Gittell et al., *School Decentralization*, p. 80.

[4] Adam Walinsky, "Review of 'Maximum Feasible Misunderstanding,'" *New York Times Book Review*, February 2, 1969, section 7.

contrast to equivalent income groups in Massachusetts's towns who send 83.9 percent of their children to public elementary schools.[5] The children of high-income parents "opt out" for other educational opportunities. During the past several years there have been many studies of large city school systems with similar findings by analysts of different perspectives. Let us briefly summarize major observations and prescriptions for reform.

Diagnosis. Virtually all analysts have concluded that America's big city school systems are inefficient and unresponsive to citizens' demands. These systems are very large: New York City, for example, has more than one million students, 60,000 teachers and 900 public schools. In these large systems there is little or no connection between voting for a school board member, or a mayor who appoints school board members, and what happens in local schools. Analysts of the larger systems have concluded that even school boards exercise little or no authority over the operation of the school systems. Citizen expression of demand must take place, if it takes place at all, through informal channels. Many parents do not have any voice in the formal educational experience of their children. Some large cities like New York have introduced some decentralization, including elected community boards. However, the maintenance of control over both finance and personnel is still in the chief administrator's office. The community boards have little to do and no authority over crucial policy areas.

In addition to problems of indicating citizen preferences, analysts of the larger systems have described a series of related problems in production and management. First, the larger systems have been found to be dominated by professional educators who ignore directives from elected or appointed officials. The combination of professionalization and unionization has put organized teachers in the position of a monopolist of the most important factor market—the labor market—making them relatively invulnerable to the directives of elected officials. Strong professionalization is not undesirable when professional educators respond to the interest of students in a way that will enhance their life prospects. However, teachers' actions in New York City have been described as "a reflection of their need to maintain the system which protects their interests."[6] They are not client oriented. Teachers come primarily from middle income

---

[5] Martin T. Katzman, *The Political Economy of Urban Schools* (Cambridge: Harvard University Press, 1971), p. 145.

[6] Gittell, *Educating an Urban Population*, p. 231.

groups with strong commitments to preparation for those life styles. Citizens of different race, ethnic backgrounds or income levels may perceive educational needs quite differently.

An ability to introduce innovative educational programs has been identified as inversely correlated with school district size over the upper size range. Large school systems are inflexible, lack innovation and do not adapt to changing conditions and changing student needs. Change in the performance of big school systems usually is the result of shocks generated outside the system. Internal influences for change at any organization level are too weak to modify a rigid system.[7]

In addition to research on the general operation of big city school systems, massive research on educational processes and educational outcomes has been done.[8] The conclusions of these studies can be very briefly summarized: First, "research has not identified a variant of existing instructional practices that is consistently related to student achievements." Individual students respond variously to different inputs. Secondly, "increasing expenditures on traditional educational practices are not likely to improve education outcomes substantially. Thus, there seem to be opportunities for a significant redirection of education expenditures without deterioration in educational outcomes." When these observations are combined with the observation of large system performance (that innovation, responsiveness and adaptation in school systems decrease with size and depend upon exogenous shocks to the system) the general conclusion is that improvement in student achievement "may require substantial changes in the organization, structure and conduct of educational experience."[9]

Prescriptions for education. Three major kinds of reform are being recommended for educational systems by independent analysts and some professional educators. These reforms include decentralization or breaking up of large school districts into smaller units, performance

---

[7] Harvey A. Averch et al., *How Effective Is Schooling? A Critical Review and Synthesis of Research Findings*, Final Report to the President's Commission on School Finances (Santa Monica, Calif.: RAND Corporation, 1971), Chapter 8.

[8] An excellent summary of the state of educational research is Averch, *How Effective Is Schooling?* Christopher Jencks et al., *Inequality: A Reassessment of the Effect of Family and Schooling in America* (New York: Basic Books, 1972) also provides a good summary but implications may be overstated in some instances.

[9] These conclusions are as summarized in Averch, *How Effective Is Schooling?* Chapter 8, pp. x, xiii. They are consistent with Jencks, *Inequality*, and nearly all other overall evaluations of education.

contracting and voucher systems. All would have some effect toward breaking up the larger districts and reducing the power of professional educators vis-à-vis administrators and elected officials. Voucher systems would, in addition, greatly strengthen the parents' role in determining the education that their children receive. Most professional educators prefer changes within the existing system, open classrooms, ungraded learning, special on-the-street learning environments and alternative schools.

Decentralization.[10] Proponents of decentralization simply argue that big city school systems are too large and they should be broken up into smaller systems serving the children in more homogeneous neighborhoods. Accompanying decentralization would be expanded area-wide or state-wide financing so that poorer districts would be able to provide a greater level of support for education. Wealthier districts would be free to tax at higher rates and provide more educational inputs above that general level. Decentralized school districts, it is argued, would give center city residents control over their own schools such as that presently enjoyed by suburban residents.

Even though concern for schools has been a major impetus to the growing community control effort, little effective decentralization has been carried out in big city systems. However, a study of one city where partial decentralization has been tried indicates that the higher citizen satisfaction with schools in the decentralized parts of the system is most probably the result of the decentralization rather than such factors as race or age.[11]

Performance contracting.[12] Performance contracting consists of a school district letting a contract to a profit or nonprofit firm for instructional services, with payment based on the achievement of students. Performance contracting is supposed to introduce an element of accountability into the educational process, with instructors strongly motivated to raise the achievement level of their students. Contract renewal is contingent on results.

What limited experience there has been with performance contracting is mixed. Many of the firms entering the field are subsidiaries of textbook publishers or manufacturers of instructional materials. As with other educational techniques, it seems to work for some

---

[10] Gittell et al., *School Decentralization*, present this view.

[11] Ernest G. Noack, "The Satisfaction of Parents with Their Community Schools as a Measure of Effectiveness of the Decentralization of a School System," *The Journal of Educational Research*, vol. 65 (April 1972), pp. 335-365.

[12] M. B. Carpenter and G. R. Hall, *Case Studies in Educational Performance Contracting: Conclusions and Implications* (Santa Monica, Calif.: RAND Corporation, 1971).

but not all students. Performance contracting does not automatically resolve the issues of citizen demand, although if used on a wide scale, it would certainly reduce the relative power of educational bureaucracies. Whether it will be successful over a long period remains to be seen.

Voucher systems.[13] Voucher systems represent the most radical proposal for change from existing educational practices. Under such a system, parents would be given vouchers to be used as credit at the schools they wished their children to attend. They could select from among all schools which met minimum standards of certification and did not discriminate on the basis of race or religion. Many variants of voucher systems have been proposed, but the essential element is that parental and student choice would lead to competition among schools as producers of educational services. Those which students and parents like, *on whatever criteria parents and children felt were important to them,* would attract students. Schools which did not perform up to student and parental expectations, again on whatever basis students and parents used, would face the potential of losing business. Vouchers, needless to say, are not welcome prospects for many educators in big city school systems. Voucher systems would deal with problems of expressing demand and monopolistic bureaucracies simultaneously. Students and parents could choose from among alternatives presented. If large systems were unmanageable, only smaller systems or even privately run schools would survive in the long run.

One of the interesting aspects of voucher proposals is the vehemence with which many professional educators have resisted them. Even more interesting, however, is the rationale for the opposition: that voucher systems would mean the demise of the public school system.[14] One can understand a reluctance to have one's monopoly positions challenged. But to admit openly that public school systems cannot compete with other alternatives in attracting

---

[13] Vouchers were first proposed by Milton Friedman in "The Role of Government in Education," in Robert A. Solow, ed., *Economics and the Public Interest* (New Brunswick, New Jersey: Rutgers University Press, 1955). The most recent comprehensive analysis is contained in *Education Vouchers: A Report on Financing Elementary Education by Grants to Parents* (Cambridge: Center for the Study of Public Policy, 1970). For a decision of the U.S. Supreme Court which seems to bar the use of vouchers for payments to sectarian schools, see *Committee for Public Education and Religious Liberty* v. *Nyquist,* 37 L Ed 2nd (1973), p. ...
[14] Ed Willingham, "Education Report/OEO Goes Ahead with Voucher Plans Despite Opposition from Teacher Groups," *National Journal* (May 1, 1971), pp. 939-946.

students is an indication of how poorly professional educators evaluate their own current performance and ability to improve future performance.

There are reasons to believe that the introduction of a voucher system would not be as disastrous for public schools as many opponents of vouchers have predicted. The first voucher experiment in the United States began in Alum Rock School District near San Jose, California during the 1972-73 school year. While no formal evaluation of the experiment will be undertaken until after the second year of operation, participants during the first year describe it as resulting in "less absenteeism and vandalism, more variety in educational offerings, more enthusiasm for school on all sides." [15] While only six public elementary schools participated in the experiment during the first year, they developed twenty-two separate "minischool" programs ranging from the traditional Three Rs to a program at Meyer Elementary School where all subjects are taught in the context of concerns with ecology and space exploration. Each elementary school can house different combinations of minischool programs.

Parental response to the first year of the experiment was mixed: 50 percent selected nontraditional programs but only 3 percent sent their children out of their neighborhood to school. For 1973-74 seven new schools have been added to the experiment, bringing the total to thirteen schools with forty-five minischool programs. Registration for 1973-74 indicates that parents are very interested in using their opportunity to select different school programs for their children: over 70 percent registered their children prior to the summer deadline and 40 percent of the parents with two or more children picked different kinds of programs for them. Twenty-five percent of the children are also enrolled in schools outside their neighborhood.[16] While a formal evaluation must wait, preliminary indications are that public school systems *can* respond to provide innovative and interesting programs for students, if the appropriate incentives exist.

Big city school systems are not performing well even though they come close to the traditional reform model for a consolidated system. The systems are large, professionalized and headed by a single appointed superintendent with a minimum of "interference" by elected or appointed school board members. The causes of problems as identified by most analysts are the very features which the advo-

---

[15] Evans Jenkins, "School Voucher Experiment Rates an 'A' in Coast District," *New York Times*, May 29, 1973, p. C54.

[16] Jack McCurdy, "School Voucher: Disputed Idea Proves Itself," *Los Angeles Times*, July 5, 1973, part 1, p. 1.

cates of traditional reform have recommended—professionalization, large scale, and uniformity.

Police Services

According to many polls and surveys, high levels of crime, especially in large cities, are of considerable concern to most citizens. While there is much disagreement as to just what changes in the FBI *Uniform Crime Reports* indicate, independent victimization surveys have shown rising levels of criminal activity in most places. Also, crime rates are higher in big cities, and within big cities crime rates are highest in slum and low-income neighborhoods. For example, in one survey of two large cities, 48 percent of the citizens indicated that they stay off the streets at night for fear of physical assault.

Reform in the criminal justice system to achieve a safer society has been the subject of a number of recent reports.[17] Our concern here, however, is with police services only. Police services are but one part of the criminal justice system, but the provision of police services is a very important function of local governments. There have been many recommendations for reforms to improve police services and thus reduce criminal activity.

The major service provided by police is generally thought to be fighting crime through prevention efforts and the apprehension of criminals. However, policemen perform a wide range of services in most communities. They are called upon to mediate family and neighborhood squabbles, patrol traffic, respond to emergency calls and perform many other services—most of which are not reflected in FBI *Uniform Crime Reports*.[18] Many people call upon police when they face critical problems which they cannot handle by themselves. Police do much more than fight crime; they help maintain the peace and security of community life.

In light of the policeman's potentially close, personal relationships with citizens, the alienation and dissatisfaction felt by some groups toward police can become a problem. When police are viewed as an "occupying force" rather than as a source of potential assis-

---

[17] Recent reports include *The Challenge of Crime in a Free Society*, a report by the President's Commission on Law Enforcement and Administration of Justice (Washington, D. C.: U.S. Government Printing Office, 1967); Committee for Economic Development, *Reducing Crime and Administering Justice* (New York, 1972); Advisory Commission on Intergovernmental Relations, *Police Reform* (Washington, D. C.: U.S. Government Printing Office, 1971).

[18] The President's Commission, *The Challenge of Crime*, Chapter 4.

tance, the general usefulness of police to the community is reduced and poor citizen-police relations greatly decrease the ability of the police to fight crime. The fight against crime also depends upon the eyes, ears and efforts of concerned citizens.

As with other local government services, costs of police services have risen sharply. Most of the costs are for personnel. Pressure to recruit "good" policemen creates demands for increased salaries even if there is little in the way of increased productivity or efficiency.

Reform prescriptions. The problems of crime, citizen alienation and rising costs are all issues which must be dealt with in order to provide better public safety. Just what are the prescriptions to resolve these problems? There have been several commission reports and studies of police services during the past few years. The conclusions emerging from the studies, however, are quite similar:[19]

(1) Police departments must have more specific guidelines for officers in the field. Departments must have relatively uniform responses which fall within guidelines set by courts and good police practices. Departments must have strong central control to achieve these objectives.

(2) Personnel must be upgraded. More college graduates should be recruited. Better in-service training must be provided. Lateral entry should be permitted for college graduates. Broadly educated community relations specialists should be hired to assume more of the policeman's duties related to emergency calls and street patrol.

(3) Fragmentation of police jurisdictions must be reduced. Many departments are too small and better coordination or integration is needed to police metropolitan areas. Criminals are not restrained by local government boundaries; police must not be either. Larger departments would be able to afford better personnel and would have greater efficiency.

(4) State governments should enact minimum statewide standards for police services. Only in this way can the negative consequences from jurisdictions with inadequate police services be eliminated.

In spite of the similarity of recommendations emerging from many commissions and studies, there is virtually no evidence that

---

[19] The President's Commission, *The Challenge of Crime*; Committee for Economic Development, *Reducing Crime and Administering Justice*; and ACIR, *Police Reform*, are all representative in this regard.

these proposed solutions will cure the problems. The President's Commission on Law Enforcement and the Administration of Justice found no apparent correlation between the number of police on the one hand, and crime rates and apprehension of criminals on the other. There is some data to indicate that quicker response time does result in higher apprehension rates, and there is a general feeling that increases in street patrols are more effective than alternative policies for reducing street crimes. A reader new to the analysis of police services will be surprised at the definiteness of recommendations with virtually no evidence supporting them. The recommendations are much more the product of a "way of thinking" about the problem—the reform tradition supporting consolidated and integrated command structures headed by competent men and staffed by professionals—than an empirical analysis of problems and alternative solutions.

Empirical studies. Some recent studies have been specifically designed to test whether reform recommendations for larger, more professionalized police departments produce equal, superior or more efficient service than smaller, less professionalized departments. Evidence on these relationships is important for formulating recommendations to reduce high crime rates, citizen alienation and rising costs.

One of these studies is a reevaluation of National Opinion Research Center (NORC) data on crime and criminal victimization. While much of the data was produced for the President's commission, the commission staff did *not* analyze it to see if the commission's conclusions concerning improvement in police services were warranted by existing information. The conclusions from the reevaluation are:

(1) Crime rates are higher in larger jurisdictions.

(2) Citizen evaluation of police services is higher in suburban and small jurisdictions.

(3) For relatively similar levels of service, the cost of police services is higher in larger jurisdictions.

(4) When the multiplicity of jurisdictions in a metropolitan area is measured by the number of municipalities per 100,000 population, the greater the number of municipalities to population, the lower are per capita costs when service levels are held constant.

In summary, traditional prescriptions for organization reform of police service agencies are *not* supported by the national data collected for the President's commission. In other words, the data available to the President's commission did not support its own recommendation.[20]

In addition to the above analysis of NORC data, there have been three comparative studies of the performance of police departments in matched neighborhood areas within and without the jurisdiction of central cities in three metropolitan areas. These studies involve the comparison of police services, their costs, crime and victimization rates and citizen satisfaction with and attitudes toward police. Small suburban jurisdictions operating their own police departments were compared with similar neighborhoods in central cities matched for socioeconomic characteristics of the residents and physical characteristics of the neighborhoods.

In one study, the cities of Beech Grove, Speedway and Lawrence in Marion County, Indiana, were compared with three adjoining matched Indianapolis neighborhoods.[21] At the time of the study, Indianapolis had a large police force of 1,100 men; the suburban jurisdictions had forces of between 18 and 26 officers. While the Indianapolis force received evaluations as an excellent department, there is no single indicator on which the Indianapolis police force was rated higher by citizens in Indianapolis when compared to citizen experiences and evaluations of the smaller suburban departments. Residents in small jurisdictions consistently rated police higher on response time and police-community relations, had lower victimization rates and were more likely to have received assistance from a policeman.

The cost of police services for the suburban communities averaged $12.80 per capita as against $21.33 per capita for the Indianapolis City Police District as a whole. However, the Indianapolis Police Department allocated resources costing only $10.72 per capita to the matched neighborhoods indicating substantial redistribution of expenditures from low crime areas to high crime areas. While the suburban departments provided higher levels of service, the service cost more than the police services being provided to the matched Indianapolis neighborhoods. As a result, no conclusion can be reached from the results of this study about relative efficiency when efficiency is measured in cost-benefit terms.

---

20 Elinor Ostrom and Roger B. Parks, "Suburban Police Departments: Too Many and Too Small?" *Urban Affairs Annual Reviews*, vol. 7 (Beverly Hills, Calif.: Sage Publications, 1973), pp. 367-402.

21 Elinor Ostrom et al., *Community Organization and the Provision of Police Services*, Sage Professional Papers in Administrative and Policy Studies, '03-001 (Beverly Hills, Calif.: Sage Publications, 1973).

A major difference between the mix of police services provided by the suburban departments and the Indianapolis department was the greater relative expenditure on patrol services in the independent communities and a greater relative expenditure on management services and detective services in the Indianapolis department. In this case at least, higher professionalization and functional specialization reduced rather than enhanced overall police performance relative to less professionalized, service-oriented suburban police departments.

A second comparative study was undertaken in the Grand Rapids, Michigan area where matched neighborhoods in Grand Rapids were compared with East Grand Rapids, Kentwood and Walker.[22] The Grand Rapids police force consisted of 313 officers, the suburban forces of from 9 to 17 officers. The findings in Grand Rapids were similar to the findings in Indianapolis with one major exception: not only did the suburban departments provide higher levels of services, *but their costs were significantly lower as well,* $10.67 per capita in the suburban communities versus $16.88 in Grand Rapids.

The third comparative study is in some ways the most interesting. It involves a comparison of two poor black villages, East Chicago Heights and Phoenix, Illinois, with three matched black areas within the city of Chicago.[23]

Chicago has one of the most professional and highly paid police departments in the United States. At the time of the study, East Chicago Heights had six full-time and five part-time policemen. Phoenix had four full-time and fifteen part-time officers. Both paid approximately $400 per month for full-time police officers and $1.60 per hour for part-time officers, who served as policemen in addition to holding other regular employment. The part-time policemen had no police training except what they received from the regular full-time officers. The villages did rely on the Cook County Sheriff's Department for criminal investigation and detention services.

The conditions existing in these black villages, when compared with the Chicago neighborhood, were as far apart as one can imagine with regard to criteria normally used to identify requirements for a "good" police force. Police services were no better in the Chicago neighborhoods than in the villages, and on several measures, the

---

[22] S. T. IsHak, "Consumers' Perception of Police Performance: Consolidation vs. Deconcentration, The Case of Grand Rapids, Michigan Metropolitan Area" (Ph.D. dissertation, Indiana University, 1972).

[23] Elinor Ostrom and Gordon Whitaker, "Black Citizens and the Police: Some Effects of Community Control" (Paper presented to the 1971 Annual Meeting of the American Political Science Association, Chicago, Illinois, 1971).

village police received better ratings. The villages spent approximately $40,000 each per year for police services; the cost in Chicago for servicing similar neighborhoods was approximately $500,000 each. From these findings it seems obvious that even very poor communities can provide police services for themselves as well or better than matched neighborhoods can expect to receive from big city police departments and do so for a much lower cost.

The conclusions from the analysis of the NORC data and the three comparative studies of police performance lend no support to the prescriptions offered by the President's commission and traditional reform recommendations for how police services should be organized. In fact, *the results indicate exactly the opposite.* Proponents of decentralization no doubt will interpret the studies as "proof" that community control and good community relations are essential in police protection. The convinced advocate of consolidation may pause to wonder about the evidence upon which his recommendations are based: Is it derived from empirical analysis of police performance or inference derived strictly from his "way of thinking" about the problem? It seems clear that counting the number of police departments in any given metropolitan area and alleging that increased fragmentation and overlap produces poor performance is simply an assertion unsupported by evidence. The performance of consolidated and fragmented systems must be measured by common indicators of performance as was done in the Indianapolis, Grand Rapids and Chicago studies before worthwhile comparisons can be made.

Fire Services

Fire services do not claim a large share of the tax dollar, and there is less concern about fire than education and police services. A recent study of fire services is extremely interesting because it is one of a few recent studies specifically designed to test hypotheses derived from public choice theory.[24]

The fire service study is a comparison of the cost of providing fire services through traditional fire departments and through a private fire company which is subject to competitive exposure. If its price is not low enough or its service is unsatisfactory the private company can be replaced. The hypotheses tested by this study were that the

---

[24] Roger S. Ahlbrandt, Jr., *Municipal Fire Protection Services: Comparison of Alternative Organizational Forms*, Sage Professional Papers in Administrative and Policy Studies, 03-002 (Beverly Hills, Calif.: Sage Publications, 1973).

private fire company would seek more efficient fire protection techniques and thus produce comparable quality and quantities of service at lower cost than traditional fire departments, and that the private fire company would make greater efforts to satisfy its customers than traditional departments.

The study was done by constructing an expenditure function to predict costs for traditional fire departments to service different areas. The items taken into account included population, area served, assessed valuation, firemen's wages, the use of volunteers, the number of full-time employees, the number of fire stations and first-aid cars, housing conditions and fire insurance ratings. The coefficient of multiple determination for the function was .96. This means that 96 percent of the variance in the cost of providing fire protection by traditional fire departments is explained by the variables taken into account.

Following the construction of the expenditure function, information on the same variables for Scottsdale, Arizona were inserted into the function to predict what the costs would be if Scottsdale were served by a traditional public fire department. The prediction indicated an expected cost of $475,000 or $7.10 per capita.

Scottsdale, however, is not served by a traditional fire department. The City of Scottsdale contracts with the Rural-Metropolitan Fire Protection Company, which also serves several other cities and unincorporated areas in Arizona. The actual contract cost for the provision of fire protection to Scottsdale by Rural-Metro was $252,000 or $3.78 per capita, a cost 47 percent lower than that predicted if the area were served in the traditional manner.

Because these cost savings were quite dramatic, an effort was made to identify the specific areas of cost saving within the Rural-Metropolitan Fire Protection Company. The cost-saving innovations which were identified include:

(1) The use of "wranglers." Wranglers are fully trained firemen who work full-time for some other city department, but are on call for immediate response to a fire alarm. Wranglers represent an intermediate step between volunteer and full-time firemen. They are as qualified as full-time professionals but paid only when fighting fires. Their pay covers full compensation for time lost on their regular job.

(2) Equipment savings. The company builds or subcontracts construction of its own trucks at a 40 percent cost saving when compared with the cost of equipment in traditional fire depart-

ments. It also uses some smaller trucks. The operational saving derived by not using a large truck is sufficient to pay for a small truck in six years. The company also uses four-inch plastic hose with quarter-turn couplings, instead of the more costly and less convenient two-and-one-half-inch cotton or nylon hose with screw couplings commonly used by traditional fire departments. The use of larger hose also permits hydrant spacing to 1,300 feet instead of the usual 500 feet, with considerable cost saving in the installation of water lines. The cost saving on water lines is *in addition to* the lower cost of fire protection.

(3) Innovation. Rural-Metro spends 3 percent of its gross revenue on research and development. The company has developed a two-pump truck so that two pumps can be delivered with a single truck. The second pump can be hydraulically lifted off the truck at the site of the fire. The company has also developed a "snail," or robot fireman. The snail is activated by water pressure in an attached hose and can be radio-controlled to enter buildings, travel down corridors, climb some stairs and spray water as directed by radio from the outside.

In addition to cost savings, a comparison of Rural-Metro's annual reports with reports from traditional fire departments indicates that the private company provides city officials with better information on the costs and potential benefits of different types and levels of fire protection than do traditional fire departments. Thus, Rural-Metro is both more efficient and more responsive in providing its users with the services they prefer.

Rural-Metro is an independently owned company regulated by the Arizona State Utilities Commission. Company profits are limited to 7 percent of *sales*, thus the only way the owner can raise total profits is to raise total sales. He does this by providing fire protection at a lower cost than cities could provide for themselves through traditionally organized fire departments. The company also has a profit-sharing plan for employees which the owner-manager feels contributes to high morale and the search for improved efficiency.

Conclusions

We have looked at problems of organization related to three types of public services supplied by local governments in urban areas. This brief examination raises serious doubts that consolidation of all local services under the control of a single unit of government for each major metropolitan area will improve the responsiveness and efficiency with which public services are provided. Reliance upon alternative solutions requires that serious attention be given to contractual and intergovernmental relationships.

The analysis of fire services in Scottsdale, Arizona, for example, indicates that a municipality can realize advantages by contracting with a private firm for the production of a public service which is supplied to all residents of the municipality. A closer look at contracting as a means of providing public services is called for, along with the use of intergovernmental agreements to permit some relatively small governmental units to perform some services while calling upon larger overlapping units of government for other services. The black villages south of Chicago referred to above, for example, rely upon Cook County Sheriff's Department to provide some investigatory and detention facilities. The Indiana State Police provide crime laboratory services for Speedway, Beech Grove and Lawrence. The possibility that intergovernmental relations can facilitate cooperative efforts to take advantage of the diverse capabilities of different units of government deserves consideration. In the next chapter, we shall examine the theoretical rationale, structural incentives and potential outcomes of different kinds of intergovernmental relationships.

5

INTERGOVERNMENTAL RELATIONS

Relations between and among governmental units are extremely important in the United States.[1] The 1967 Census of Governments enumerated 81,299 separate governmental units.[2] Most analyses of intergovernmental relations have focused upon the vertical structure of federal-state relationships, state-local relationships and federal-state-local relationships. Emphasis has been upon the role of the federal government or the states in intergovernmental relationships. Very little attention has been given to the horizontal relationships that exist among the 3,049 counties, 18,048 municipalities, 17,105 townships, 21,782 school districts and 21,264 other special districts. The most numerous of these special districts are those concerned with natural resource services (6,539), fire protection (3,665), urban water supply (2,140), housing and renewal (1,565), cemeteries (774), parks and recreation (613), hospitals (537) and libraries (410). There are also more than 450 special districts classified as multi-purpose districts by the Census. Many resource-management districts also provide a wide spectrum of urban-type services. Of the 81,248 separate local government units, 17,856 are located in the 148 Standard Metropolitan Statistical Areas having populations in excess of 200,000.[3] Many

---

[1] Several parts of this chapter are abstracted from Chapter 18, "Intergovernmental Fiscal Relations," in Harold M. Groves and Robert L. Bish, *Financing Government*, 7th ed. (New York: Holt, Rinehart and Winston, 1973). The authors thank Holt, Rinehart and Winston for permission to use portions of that chapter in this monograph.

[2] U.S. Bureau of the Census, *Census of Governments, 1967: Governmental Organization*, vol. 1 (Washington, D. C.: U.S. Government Printing Office, 1968), pp. 1 and 5.

[3] Ibid., p. 10.

of these units overlap one another. While this multiplicity of jurisdictions is often criticized, there is nothing irrational or illogical about
having different public functions performed by different jurisdictions.
Different jurisdictions can provide different services in much the same
way that different private firms provide different services to people
in any given urban area.

With such a number of governmental units serving any given
urban area, one would expect that rivalry occurs and that some forms
of rivalry are detrimental to wider communities of interest. One
might also expect a number of governmental units to take advantage
of each others' capabilities and pursue mutually productive relationships through cooperative agreements, contracts and joint operating
arrangements.

The traditional reform movement favoring consolidation has
emphasized the negative consequences of competition among governmental jurisdictions. Explicit recognition that intergovernmental
agreements may be an alternative to consolidation has received increasing attention in recent studies, but such agreements are viewed
as an inferior step preparing the way for eventual consolidation.[4]
Because multiple overlapping jurisdictions are assumed to be dis-
orderly, those favoring consolidation have not explored the possibility
that intergovernmental relations may manifest an orderliness somewhat
comparable to market systems. Intergovernmental competition and
coordination through intergovernmental contracts and agreements is
quite different from coordination through hierarchical ordering. But
such competition and coordination can be both orderly and productive.

Five aspects of intergovernmental relations will be examined in
this chapter: first, tax coordination and competition; second, functional grants and contracts; third, bloc grants and revenue sharing;
fourth, conflict and conflict resolution and fifth, public service industries as a way of conceptualizing the organization of intergovernmental relationships among multiple jurisdictions. While the analysis
must be relatively brief, an understanding of the use and potential
of intergovernmental competition and cooperation for creating ordered
relationships is essential to an understanding of the urban public sector
and for the formulation of prescriptions to improve its performance.

---

[4] For example, see Advisory Commission on Intergovernmental Relations, *Alter-
native Approaches to Governmental Reorganization in Metropolitan Areas*
(Washington, D. C.: U.S. Government Printing Office, 1962), and Committee for
Economic Development, *Reshaping Government in Metropolitan Areas* (New
York, 1970).

Tax Competition and Cooperation

There are two basic types of tax competition. One type is competition for the same tax base. An implicit assumption exists that the governmental unit that gets there first preempts the base and prevents others from using it. The second type of tax competition is when adjacent jurisdictions keep taxes low to compete for desired industries or residents.

Both aspects of tax competition may keep taxes down. Both are alleged to be undesirable by state and local officials, others who advocate higher public spending and reformers who advocate greater discretion for governmental officials who are assumed to know the public interest—and thus should not be "artificially" constrained in their actions.

The heavy use of the income tax by the federal government was at one time alleged to prevent state and local governments from using this source of revenue. Thus state and local governments were relegated to the use of sales and property taxes, and hence derived a lower revenue growth rate than the federal government.[5] While state and local governments do rely on slower growing tax sources than the federal government, forty-one states and numerous local governments have adopted income taxes. In spite of heavy federal use, it is obvious that the income tax has not been preempted by the federal government.

Tax competition between adjacent jurisdictions has forced many local government officials to reconsider tax increases which would raise taxes to the detriment of local residents or businessmen in competition with those in adjacent areas. Such officials are pressed to develop more efficient uses of present revenues in lieu of tax increases. It would appear that tax competition among adjacent jurisdictions, like any kind of competition, will limit the unilateral discretion of local government officials and force them to be more efficient than they might otherwise be.

---

[5] Tax revenue growth rates are compared through the use of a concept called tax elasticity. Tax elasticity is a measure of the rate of growth in tax revenue relative to the rate of growth in income. Elastic taxes are taxes with revenue growth of a higher rate than income growth. Inelastic taxes are taxes with revenue growth which is much lower than income growth. Elastic taxes include the personal and corporate income tax. Property, sales and excise taxes are generally inelastic. Use of elastic taxes results in increasing revenues without having to raise tax rates. Reliance on inelastic taxes requires continual increases in tax rates if cost increases are to be met and any increased spending undertaken. For a detailed analysis see Groves and Bish, *Financing Government,* Chapter 17.

If government officials are always assumed to be knowledgeable and to act in the public interest, limiting their discretion would be undesirable because government officials will always be efficient. Thus tax competition, from this perspective, would be considered undesirable. If one assumes that government officials are likely to be both fallible and self-interested, the ability of citizens to exercise choice and locate in competing jurisdictions provides an incentive for local government officials to act as efficiently as possible. Many analysts would consider this type of pressure to be a desirable consequence of tax competition.

Tax coordination occurs primarily in areas of tax administration. Tax deductions or credits for taxes paid to other jurisdictions are used to resolve potential problems of double taxation or to influence the behavior of other jurisdictions. Another example of coordinated tax administration would be a case in which an individual or businessman needs to keep only one set of records for two or more governments using the same tax base, as when both state and federal income tax laws require the same information for tax purposes. Another form of coordinated tax administration occurs when one jurisdiction contracts with another for the collection of its taxes. It is quite common for state governments to collect income and sales taxes for local governments and for some local governments to collect property taxes for states and other local jurisdictions by mutual agreement. Under the Federal-State Tax Collection Act of 1972, the Internal Revenue Service may contract with states for the collection of state income taxes.

Tax deductions and tax credits [6] are often permitted for taxes paid to another jurisdiction, as when the federal government permits deductibility of taxes paid to state and local governments, when one state permits credit for income taxes paid to other states, or local governments permit credit for taxes paid to other jurisdictions. The widespread use of deductions and crediting arrangements resolves many of the problems of double taxation for persons doing business in two or more jurisdictions or individuals who reside in one jurisdiction and work in another.

The unilateral granting of deductions or credits by the federal or state governments for taxes paid smaller governments can also be used to encourage or discourage smaller units of government from using specific taxes. This permits the larger unit, which represents a

---

[6] Tax deductions are deductions from income of taxes paid elsewhere in determining the tax base upon which tax liability is calculated. Tax credits are subtractions of taxes paid elsewhere from taxes owed.

broader constituency, to influence smaller units to take account of the broader community of interest.[7]

Functional Grants

Functional grants are payments by one level of government to a lower level of government for which the recipient unit undertakes activities agreed upon by the grantee and grantor. While called "grants," functional grants are essentially contracts under which one government purchases the performance of a service under stipulated conditions from the grantee or pays to get the grantee to undertake specific activities. Both federal and state functional grant programs are large. In fiscal 1971 the federal government granted $27.5 billion to state and local units. This was equal to 15.5 percent of federal expenditures and approximately 19 percent of state and local government receipts. In 1970-71, state governments granted local governments $32.6 billion in functional grants, an amount nearly equal to 37 percent of state expenditures and approximately 35 percent of local government receipts.[8]

The rationale behind functional grants at both the state and federal level is quite clear: the larger unit, representing a larger and different constituency than the smaller unit, has determined that an increased or modified output of some locally produced good or service is desirable. It proceeds to pay grantee units to increase or modify their output of that good or service, often requiring local matching funds or conformance to program performance standards to insure net increases or modifications in outputs rather than simply substitution of federal or state funds for local funds. The granting unit usually has the legal authority to produce the desired services itself. However, in a great number of cases, it is more efficient for the

---

[7] Two uses of tax credits to induce uniformity are the federal government's 80 percent credit for death taxes paid to state governments to encourage all states to impose death taxes. Prior to imposition of the federal tax, Nevada and Florida had no death taxes to attract retired residents to their states. Nevada still has no death tax, although a state tax of 80 percent of the federal rates would cost state residents nothing. Another example of tax credits to achieve uniformity is California's crediting of 1 point of a 5 percent sales tax to local governments if, but only if, the local governments impose a 1 percent sales tax. If a local government preferred a 2 percent sales tax, citizens would not get the state tax credit and thus would end up paying 7 percent. This provision has led to uniform adoption of local government 1 percent sales tax and total sales tax of 5 percent throughout the state—except for the San Francisco Bay area, where additional taxes are used to support mass transit.

[8] U.S. Bureau of the Census, *Governmental Finances in 1970-71* (Washington, D. C.: U.S. Government Printing Office, 1972), Tables 16 and 17.

grantor to contract with the grantee to produce an appropriate mix of the desired service. In this way the financial resources of the larger unit can be combined with decentralized production by smaller units to accomplish policies desired by the larger units.[9]

Prior to the shakeup of federal functional grant programs in 1973, the federal government had over 400 such programs. Eighty percent of the funds were concentrated in education, highways and public welfare. State governments also have a variety of programs, but in the aggregate, 87 percent of state funds go to local governments for the same types of services that are supported by the federal government.

Education, highways and public welfare are all areas in which benefits from local expenditures may spill over the boundaries of local or even state jurisdictions yet local production of specific services is most efficient. Education spillovers may occur because children educated in one district often migrate to other areas. Some minimum level of education is considered desirable by future employers and neighbors no matter how poor the school district where children were reared may have been. Even though financing is provided by large units to take account of the favorable spillover effects produced by education, it still appears most efficient to permit smaller local units to undertake the actual production of educational services.

Highways are another area where benefits may spill over to users from outside the jurisdiction undertaking highway construction and maintenance. Thus, the federal government finances virtually all expenditures for the construction of the interstate system, with state highway departments responsible for construction and maintenance. The federal government represents the nation's highway users as buyers of highway services. State highway departments produce highways and highway maintenance. Given variations in geographic and climatic conditions, it is doubtful that a federal agency could build and maintain highways more economically than states. Local governments are left to provide their own local roads and streets where benefits are primarily enjoyed by local citizens, although there is some supplemental funding from state and federal sources. This interjurisdictional cooperation produces a network of highways, roads and streets that serve many different communities of interest.

Public welfare presents a somewhat different problem than education or highways. It is in the joint interest of citizens in any single

---

[9] Selma J. Mushkin and John F. Cotton, *Sharing Federal Funds for State and Local Needs* (New York: Praeger, 1969), provides a good analysis of the development of federal grant programs.

local unit of government to avoid income redistribution programs, even if each individual citizen desires redistribution, so long as other governmental units provide such programs. Any attempt by a small unit to undertake income redistribution creates the potential for a dual migration problem, with high-income families moving to locations where less redistribution is undertaken and low-income families moving to areas with high levels of income redistribution.[10] As governmental units grow, covering larger areas, migration becomes more costly. Thus financing of welfare and other highly redistributive activities has tended to shift from local, to state, to national government.[11]

Functional grant programs are often criticized on two bases, and they have one inherent problem that has not been resolved. The first criticism is that they are extremely complex. The second is that they distort local priorities. The answer to the second criticism is quite simple. Of course they distort local priorities. Grants were specifically designed to get local units to undertake actions they would not otherwise have undertaken.

The complexity of the grant programs is a more difficult issue. They were never intended to be an integrated program; they are ad hoc responses to specific problems where different constituencies share different communities of interest by access through different levels of government. From the perspective of any one local government official, the 400-plus federal programs can be confusing. Unless diverse local agencies can take advantage of grants, then grantsmanship may become a game which either wastes local funds or leads some officials to neglect grant opportunities from which there would be mutual benefits. National officials as buyers of public services produced by state and local agencies may also have confused "grants" with philanthropy rather than as payments for services to be procured in accordance with national interests.

When grants are viewed as a form of government philanthropy, some peculiar patterns of behavior become manifest. Instead of helping local officials solve problems, officials of some granting agencies

---

[10] It should be noted that families do not have to move in specific response to dissatisfaction with the public provision of services or local government financing of income redistribution. In a society where approximately 20 percent of all families change their residential location each year all that is necessary is that families take into account public goods and services and local government taxes when selecting a new residential location.

[11] Many grants contain equalization features in their formula. However, empirical studies of grant distributions indicate very little income redistribution actually occurs because other elements in the formula wipe out the equalizing effects. Distributional consequences of functional grants are essentially random.

develop an arm's length coyness in giving ambiguous suggestions to local officials on how to plan, draft and rewrite grant applications. An inordinate amount of time and paper work can be required while agency representatives carefully reserve decisions for higher officials about whether to make the grant or reject the application. Abrupt shifts in policies occur, and the burden of those shifts largely falls upon the potential recipients. The confusion of grants with philanthropy can evoke substantial frustration and ill-will.

When grants are viewed as payments for services rendered to meet the preferences of national constituencies, it is important for federal officials to act as aggressive purchasing agents providing local officials with information on grant programs. Performance depends upon adequate information and a clarification of what service standards are of relevance to national constituencies. Purchasing agents are following a rational strategy if they can help vendors meet specifications and produce satisfactory services.

A recent major study of federal grant programs does conclude that some packaging would improve the efficiency of grant programs, but still concludes that many specific programs are needed if national interests are to be properly taken into account.[12] The alternatives are either increased national production of public goods and services now produced by state and local agencies or a failure to generate a mix of locally produced public goods and services which meets the preference of national users of those goods and services.

When considering budgets for higher education, citizens and state legislators in any particular state have little reason to make substantial investments in, for example, foreign language training programs. When considering national security matters, the same citizens probably would give a higher priority to language training as an object of federal expenditures. The federal government might rationally decide to use these funds to buy increased language training capabilities to be supplied by state universities and colleges. Lack of an opportunity to do so might lead to the development of specialized federal language training institutions apart from state universities and colleges.

An unresolved problem with grant programs is that which occurs with the creation of any political authority. The authority necessary for public officials to "do good" also permits them to "do bad." Legislative authority to permit efficient achievement of widely shared national or state objectives can also be used to open the treasury to

---

[12] Mushkin and Cotton, *Sharing Federal Funds.*

raids by well-organized interest groups. Usually, no single interest group will take large enough sums for legislators or citizens in general to be greatly concerned. But together, the accumulated raids of all interest groups may involve large sums of money.

The Constitution created a system of overlapping jurisdictions specifically so that minorities within one jurisdiction could carry their problems to another jurisdiction reflecting different communities of interest. This was the basis for Madison's solution to the problem of majority tyranny. Functional grants have contributed greatly to the openness of the American political system, and it is difficult, if not impossible, to conclude that elimination of functional grants would offer a net improvement. This is not to say that the present system cannot be improved. Modifications in particular grant programs would certainly be justified; but an abandonment of conditional grant programs in general would cause serious dislocation in the mix of public goods and services currently produced by state and local agencies.

Service Contracts

Intergovernmental contracts constitute a means for purchasing public goods and services by one governmental unit from another governmental unit. Contracts are also let to private firms for the production of public goods and services, as in the case of Scottsdale's purchase of fire services from the Rural-Metropolitan Fire Protection Company. Contracts are most common among local governments although state and federal agencies sometimes participate in buying and selling public services. The U.S. Army Corps of Engineers, for example, contracts with state and local agencies to produce a variety of water services.

The major use of service contracts occurs when a relatively small unit purchases a public good or service from a larger unit because the larger unit has lower costs of production and can sell to the smaller unit at a lower price than it would cost the smaller unit to produce the service for itself. At the same time, the smaller unit is able to specify the quantity or quality of the service to be provided, and thus citizen preferences are met more closely than would be the case if the small unit were simply merged with the larger unit.

A common type of intergovernmental contracting involves the purchase of police services from a larger city or county by a small community. Even medium-sized cities with their own police forces enter into contractual arrangements with larger jurisdictions to secure communication services, crime lab services, jail facilities and police training services. The diversity in the nature of public goods and services means that different kinds of services are produced efficiently by different-sized jurisdictions. Contracting permits relatively small jurisdictions, through which citizens can indicate their preferences more precisely than is possible in larger units, to obtain the advantages of lower cost production when economies of scale accrue in the production of some types of public goods or services. If a single unit of government must serve both to articulate preferences and produce a full range of municipal public goods and services, it will be either too large to perform some services efficiently or too small to produce other goods and services at low cost. With adjustments through the use of contracts, many different goods and services can be provided more efficiently and more responsively at the same time.

An extreme form of contracting, called the "Lakewood Plan," is used by many California cities. Lakewood, California (approximately 80,000 population) was incorporated in 1953 to avoid annexation by Long Beach. Lakewood's citizens felt that they would be better able to get the public services they desired through their own city rather than by being annexed to a larger city. The city began with only ten employees and relied upon special districts and contracts, primarily with Los Angeles County, for most of its municipal services. Police services, animal control, engineering services, street maintenance and other functions were provided under contract with the county. Following Lakewood's example, twenty-five other cities incorporated in Los Angeles County between 1954 and 1961, all relying primarily on contract services rather than becoming independent producers of local municipal services. Since that time contract cities have been organized in other urban areas of California.[13] Contracting for services among municipalities is also commonplace in other metropolitan areas in many parts of the United States.

We have already observed how contracting for fire protection services in Scottsdale led to greater responsiveness, lower cost and increased provision of information on costs and benefits for different levels and kinds of fire protection services. Some of these consequences have been observed to result from intergovernmental contracting as well. A major observed consequence of the Lakewood Plan is that the county as the producer is forced to measure and cost-out all services provided—a rather unusual procedure for govern-

---

[13] For an analysis of Lakewood Plan development, see Robert Warren, *Government in Metropolitan Regions: A Reappraisal of Fractionated Political Organization* (Davis: Institute of Governmental Affairs, University of California, 1966). For an analysis of information and market-type incentives, see Robert Warren, "A Municipal Services Market Model of Metropolitan Organization," *Journal of the American Institute of Planners,* vol. 30 (August 1964) pp. 193-204.

ments—and then offer a price lower than that at which a city could produce a service for itself. Cities have also encouraged private producers and adjacent municipalities to bid for contract services. Such efforts have brought lower prices and consequently forced cost-saving innovations among public producers. Contract producers are exposed to potential competition and run the risk of losing customers. At the same time, small cities receive benefits from lower-cost production. They are also able to adjust service levels to meet the needs of their citizens. It appears that contract systems contain within them incentives for responsiveness to diverse preferences, incentives to keep costs of production down and an ability to adjust production economies to produce diverse public goods and services more efficiently.

The multiplicity of governments and intergovernmental agreements in metropolitan areas may appear "chaotic" or incomprehensible to some observers who assume that coordination can be achieved only through hierarchical structures. When the diverse nature of public goods and services and the difficulty of meeting diverse demands of citizens through large-scale bureaucracies are recognized, the complex governmental systems existing in many metropolitan areas appear to be not only rational but to be *an essential prerequisite* for an efficient and responsive performance in the public sector.[14] The essential rationality of the orderly relationships which exist among many governmental units within metropolitan areas has only been recognized over the past decade by a limited number of analysts. However, empirical research on the comparative performance of alternative institutional arrangements has not yet been undertaken on a sufficiently broad scale to provide firm evidence about the relative advantage of different structures.

Bloc Grants and Revenue Sharing

Bloc grants are simple cash transfers from one government to another according to a formula that is not related to the performance of a specific service. The recipient unit can spend the grant money at its own discretion. About 13 percent of state grants to local government are of the bloc-grant type. Formulas for bloc grants usually include a per capita component, and are sometimes adjusted by income or wealth to achieve some income redistribution. Bloc grants differ from

---

[14] For an early recognition of these issues see Vincent Ostrom, Charles Tiebout and Robert Warren, "The Organization of Government in Metropolitan Areas: A Theoretical Inquiry," *American Political Science Review*, vol. 60 (December 1961), pp. 831-842.

shared taxes in that formulas for distribution are not based on the origin of the funds by jurisdiction. However, revenues collected and distributed under bloc grant formulas often have their origins in a system of shared taxes.

The new federal revenue sharing program introduced in 1972 is like many state bloc-grant programs under which an allocated amount is distributed among state and local governments.[15] The amount of the first five-year appropriation is slightly over $30 billion. The distribution formula includes elements of population, revenue effort by state and local governments, income, urbanization and state and federal individual income tax collections in a state.[16] Because there are per capita and income elements in the formula, and because higher amounts of federal income taxes are collected in high-income states, some income redistribution is expected to result. However, the addition of the revenue effort factor provides additional funds to those jurisdictions taxing relatively more of their citizens' personal income for general revenues in the public sector and penalizes those states and local areas which do relatively less through expenditures of public funds or place heavier reliance upon user charges or special assessments instead of general taxes. The focus on general governments (and their general tax revenue) also discriminates against the use of special districts for functions where boundaries different from those of a general government may be most efficient. For example, if taxes collected by the Municipality of Metropolitan Seattle, an area-wide sub-county special district undertaking sewage treatment and public transportation functions, were instead collected by the county or city government, their share of revenue sharing funds would increase. The county or city could obtain still more revenue sharing funds if it financed all sewage facilities and public transit from general taxes instead of partially from user charges.

While low income-high revenue effort jurisdictions will receive relatively high per capita amounts, other low-income jurisdictions with lower revenue efforts and greater reliance upon private services and voluntary efforts—or few services at all—will receive relatively low per capita amounts of shared revenue. At the same time high

---

[15] Public Law 92-512; 86 Stat. 919. *State and Local Fiscal Assistance Act of 1972,* October 20, 1972.

[16] Actually, state shares are determined by one of two formulas, whichever provides the higher amount. One formula includes population, income and revenue effort; the other includes population, income, revenue effort, urbanization and state and federal individual income tax collections in the state. The first formula was proposed in the House, the second in the Senate; both were included in the conference committee report enacted into law.

income-low revenue effort jurisdictions will receive relatively low per capita amounts while other high-income jurisdictions with higher revenue efforts and larger expenditures for full-time paid employees will receive relatively high per capita amounts of revenue. The inclusion of a revenue effort factor may eliminate much of the income redistribution aspect of the distribution formula.

The original Nixon administration revenue sharing proposal approached a pure no-strings bloc grant. The revenue sharing legislation enacted by Congress added some "strings," but still left revenue sharing more like a bloc than a functional grant. Among the restrictions imposed by Congress are that revenue sharing funds can be used only for services designated as "priority" services by the Congress. These services are public safety, environmental protection, public transportation, health, recreation, libraries, social services for the poor or aged, financial administration and capital construction. Education is noticeably omitted. Revenue sharing funds cannot be used to match other functional federal grants. Additional requirements include anti-discrimination clauses, administration through trust funds, administration of fiscal operations within guidelines established by the secretary of the treasury, and wage equivalency with private construction, as determined by the secretary of labor, for capital construction undertaken with 25 percent or more shared revenue funds.

While revenue sharing in the form of bloc grants has been used by state governments for a long time, federal revenue sharing through bloc grants has generated a high level of controversy. As with many other government policies, it was easier to get agreement on establishment of a revenue sharing program than it has been to obtain a consensus on how it should be used. This, of course, is consistent with a situation in which parties to an agreement achieve diverse and independent objectives from the same program.

Major reasons advanced in support of revenue sharing include:

(1) It would broaden the use of the rapidly growing and progressive income tax. This would relieve state and local governments of the need to rely heavily on slow-growing and regressive taxes. From this perspective, revenue sharing is viewed as simply a shared use of the same tax, as states have been doing with local governments for a long time. States could also take advantage of the income tax collecting machinery already available to the federal government through the Internal Revenue Service.

(2) It would strengthen state and local governments per se. Seen in this light, revenue sharing is serving a specific function, like

functional grant programs. The function is implementation of a national policy to strengthen state and local governments. Some proponents would use revenue sharing to "strengthen" state and local governments by requiring states to submit plans for accomplishing objectives such as the consolidation of local governments, reliance upon a short ballot with few elected officials, a single strong executive, et cetera.[17] The program of traditional advocates of consolidation would, under these conditions, be made the object of federal revenue sharing.

Opponents of revenue share have differing perspectives as well. Individuals who oppose progressive taxation and rapidly growing taxes in general oppose revenue sharing instead of the use of other types of taxation or reduced government spending. Others feel that state and local governments need to be strengthened, but they argue that strength comes from efficiently producing goods and services that respond to their citizens' preferences as reflected in their willingness to pay. It may be because state and local governments are not closely responsive to citizen preferences that citizens do not want to pay higher taxes. Providing these governments with additional revenue from the federal treasury will not make them any more responsive or more efficient. Individuals with this perspective also might argue that it is better for the federal government to cut taxes if revenues are in excess of that needed for federal programs. Then, if citizens wished, they could pay higher taxes to state and local units without the federal government making those decisions for them.

The recommendation to use revenue sharing to force consolidation of local governments with the expectation that consolidation and external financing will "strengthen" local government deserves special comment in an analysis comparing reform through consolidation with public choice approaches to public sector analysis. Public choice analysts would agree that consolidations and external funding would "strengthen" the monopoly power of local government officials in relation to citizens. Thus, that strength may well be used to ignore citizen needs and preferences instead of satisfying them. From the public choice perspective, the use of revenue sharing to force consolidation of local governments would be counter-productive if the objective is to increase the responsiveness of local governments to their citizens.

---

[17] Henry S. Reuss, *Revenue Sharing: Crutch or Catalyst for State and Local Governments* (New York: Praeger, 1970).

Others are less concerned with revenue sharing per se than with "special" revenue sharing proposals intended to repackage functional grants into broad categories. Functional grant programs, as indicated earlier, have provided diverse groups with access to governmental support to assist them with special problems. If these programs involve national constituencies with interests that are not adequately represented by state and local officials, then these groups would predict that many justifiable and desirable programs will be eliminated if local government officials make allocational decisions without regard for external interests. At the same time, of course, some raids on the federal treasury would be halted.

Other scholars predict that revenue sharing will improve local fiscal administration through application of federal requirements and provide local governments, especially smaller units, with more fiscal resources to respond to local needs.[18]

In conclusion, the effect of revenue sharing should be to at least partially increase the growth of revenues of local governments, thus making their financial crises less severe. However, we do not expect increased responsiveness and efficiency from local governments to accrue from bloc grants. One might view revenue sharing, harshly but realistically, as a new raid on the federal treasury, a raid by state and local government officials who find it easier to convince congressmen that they need more funds than to convince their local constituents that the benefits from additional taxes will exceed costs.

On the other hand, substantial advantages can accrue from reliance upon the tax collecting machinery of the federal government to collect income taxes. Working out appropriate relationships to take advantage of federal tax collecting capabilities and, at the same time, establishing appropriate expenditure policies at different levels of government will require careful analysis, practical experience and critical scrutiny of that experience. We cannot hope to resolve this issue in this monograph. We can only emphasize the diverse communities of interest and the many units of government that need to be considered in the development of expenditure policies in a complex public economy. Expenditure policies are critical in determining the

---

18 Two analysts who have reached these conclusions are: Murray L. Weidenbaum, a major formulator of the Nixon administration proposal ("Revenue Sharing and the Federal System," paper presented to the Conference on Adjusting to the New Federalism, University of North Carolina at Chapel Hill, June 25, 1973), and Edward A. Lutz ("In Support of a New Approach to State-Local Relationships in New York State," paper for the Special Study Committee of the County Officers Association, March 1972).

mix of different public goods and services provided by all different units of government.

Conflict and Conflict Resolution

Conflict is often viewed as something to be avoided. However, competition and a potential for conflict always exist when individuals must share a common environment and supply of resources. Unless conflict can be constrained and processed in an orderly way, a danger exists for it to escalate into interjurisdictional warfare in which everyone would be left worse off. On the other hand, conflict can serve a constructive educational purpose when human beings are not fully aware of all the consequences which flow from their actions. When actions harm others, those who are injured need institutional facilities such as courts where the merits of their claims will be considered and conflicts resolved. Conflict and methods for conflict resolution provide arrangements where differing viewpoints can be fully assessed and where it is possible for individuals to reappraise their actions in relation to the actions of others in light of fuller information. These reappraisals will often lead to the discovery of new mutually beneficial solutions to conflicts, something that would not occur if one viewpoint is arbitrarily imposed.

If local government jurisdictions were petty "Balkan" states, interjurisdictional warfare would be as endemic as warfare in the Middle East. The basic reason for developing the American federal system was to avoid the phenomenon of Balkanization. Each unit of government is presumed to be independent in providing for its own self-government in accordance with republican principles of popular control. However, the concept of a federal system implies that overlapping jurisdictions will exist so that larger jurisdictions—sometimes called higher levels of government—will provide institutional facilities for processing conflicts and resolving controversies which may arise among smaller jurisdictions.

Various institutional arrangements exist at different levels of government for resolving conflicts that may arise at other levels of government. De Tocqueville long ago recognized that the American system of public administration relied heavily upon independent officials who are controlled more by processes of popular election and by recourse to courts of law than by a single overarching hierarchy of public authority.[19] Government officials can be held

19 Alexis de Tocqueville, *Democracy in America*, vol. 1 (New York: Random House, 1945), pp. 76-77.

accountable to rules of law where the judiciary can be used to enforce claims of citizens against them or where one governmental jurisdiction can challenge the actions of other governmental jurisdictions which it considers injurious to its interests. These remedies are available through both state and federal courts.

Similarly, state legislatures and Congress, within the constraints of their respective constitutions, have authority to enact legislation to alter the basic rules of law that apply to the conduct of public affairs among local governmental jurisdictions. The organization of most types of local governmental jurisdictions occurs under legislation enacted by state legislatures. Congress has broad authority to regulate affairs that impinge upon interstate interests. Both state and federal administrative agencies provide a significant range of public services to the residents of every urban area. Area-wide highway systems are financed, developed and maintained by the coordinated actions of federal and state agencies. State police provide area-wide police services, including area-wide traffic patrol in most metropolitan regions. The U.S. Postal Service provides area-wide postal services in each community and metropolitan area as well as for the nation as a whole.

The decision-making arrangements and administrative facilities provided by state and federal governments form a part of the super-structure for the government of each metropolitan area. They provide the means for processing conflicts and for searching out resolutions to conflict so as to avoid interjurisdictional warfare.

Balkanization in American local government is largely an illusion created by ways of thinking which associate chaos with overlapping jurisdictions and fragmentation of authority. Federal systems of government necessarily involve overlapping jurisdictions. Separation of powers necessarily involves fragmentation of authority.

Most metropolitan areas have a rich structure of both formal and informal arrangements for considering interjurisdictional problems and for working out interjurisdictional cooperation among public officials and employees who serve local areas. Costs of litigation can be high in money, time and effort expended. Costs of legislative action in the presence of strong disagreement among contending interests can also involve large expenditures in money, time and effort. Under such circumstances, public officials have incentives to reduce the frustrations of extended conflict and to seek less costly forms of conflict resolution. Informal negotiations or regular discussions organized through voluntary associations such as associations of cities and public officials become means by which most conflicts are resolved. Rational individuals have incentives to search out solutions in relation to the alternatives that are available to them. If negotiated solutions are less costly than adjudicated solutions or actions influenced by hostile legislators, then we would expect local officials in metropolitan areas to develop means to solve their problems through discussion and negotiation.

Since arrangements for discussion and negotiation are rarely mandated in legislation, those arrangements will escape notice in the public press and in scholarly studies. Yet historical research on public policy issues involving interjurisdictional problems does reveal extensive patterns of interjurisdictional cooperation.[20] Those who know the least about the detailed problems confronting public service agencies in metropolitan areas are often the ones who are most preoccupied with the dangers of interjurisdictional warfare.

Public Service Industries

The 80,000 units of government in the United States, the 1,400 governments in the New York metropolitan area and the large numbers of jurisdictions existing in most metropolitan areas can be viewed as so many different public firms or public enterprises in a public service economy. Some firms are of small size and enable people to meet service needs that occur within a relatively small neighborhood or community. Other firms are of intermediate size and enable the same people to serve the needs they share with wider communities of interest. Still other jurisdictions and firms give access to capabilities that are related to still larger communities of interest.

Each of the agencies which cooperate in providing a similar type of public service, but take account of different communities of interest, can be viewed as a public firm in a public service industry.[21] Such a view of the diverse overlapping jurisdictions can lead one to contemplate an orderly relationship among the numerous agencies forming the police industry, the education industry, the water industry, the health services industry and the transportation industry, all of which

---

[20] An interesting study of the development of the public sector in Los Angeles County is contained in Warren, *Government in Metropolitan Regions*, Chapters 4-13. The water industry, which played a crucial role in permitting urbanization of the arid Southern California region, is considered in Vincent Ostrom's study *Water and Politics* (Los Angeles: Haynes Foundation, 1953).

[21] Vincent Ostrom and Elinor Ostrom, "A Behavioral Approach to Intergovernmental Relations," *Annals of the American Academy of Political and Social Science*, vol. 359 (May 1965), pp. 137-146.

form an integral part of the public service economy in any particular metropolitan area.[22]

Many firms in a public service industry need not mean chaos. An industry perspective also facilitates the inclusion of private firms such as the Rural-Metro fire company in Scottsdale, Arizona, and voluntary associations such as leagues of cities or water users' associations as important agencies in the public economy of metropolitan areas. The illusion of the "crazy-quilt" pattern is no more than a free association stimulated by graphic patterns on maps; it is not a critical assessment of the performance of public service agencies.

Rather than assuming that a fully integrated monopoly would be the most efficient purveyor of all public goods and services in a metropolitan region, a student of industrial organization would expect that a multiplicity of agencies would be better able to take advantage of diverse economies of scale. Determining the relative efficiency of different structural arrangements among different public service industries would then be a matter for empirical investigation.

Conclusion

Patterns of tax competition, fiscal transfers associated with functional grants, interjurisdictional service contracts, revenue sharing and bloc grants, patterns of conflict and conflict resolution and the organization of trade associations among public agencies are but some of the variables that might be investigated in studies of the public economy of different metropolitan areas. We would not be surprised to find, as de Tocqueville did in the 1830s, a highly fragmented system of public administration in each metropolitan area where "uniformity or permanence of design, the minute arrangement of details, and the perfection of administrative systems must not be sought for . . .; what we find there is the presence of a power which, if it is somewhat wild, is at least robust, and an existence checkered with accident, indeed, but full of animation and effort."[23]

---

[22] Some studies consistent with this conceptualization include those in a Haynes Foundation Monograph Series, *Metropolitan Los Angeles: A Study in Integration,* including: Winston W. Crouch, Wendell MacCoby, Margaret G. Morder, and Richard Bigger, *Sanitation and Health,* 1952; James K. Trump, Morton Kroll, and James R. Donoghue, *Fire Protection,* 1952; Vincent Ostrom, *Water Supply,* 1953; and Helen L. Jones, *Libraries,* 1953. The reader is also referred to Joe S. Bain, Richard E. Caves and Julius Margolis, *Northern California's Water Industry: the Comparative Efficiency of Public Enterprise in Developing a Scarce Natural Resource* (Baltimore: The Johns Hopkins Press, 1966).

[23] de Tocqueville, *Democracy in America,* pp. 95-96.

6

THE WEIGHT OF EVIDENCE

Theory is a necessary tool for thinking about problems. No one can see the whole picture in a complex reality. As a consequence, individuals, whether scholars, citizens or officials, need simplifying concepts that enable them to reason through problems in relation to alternative courses of action. When two different theories lead to contradictory conclusions, substantial doubt is cast over the appropriateness of one or the other approach. When conditions are identified by one group of analysts as generating one set of consequences and those same conditions are viewed by other analysts as leading to different, often contradictory, consequences, we are presented with a difficult problem in deciding what to believe.

Policy analysts who propose different solutions to the problem of urban government have based their analyses, at least in part, upon contradictory positions. The older reform tradition proposing consolidation bases its assessment on presumptions that overlapping jurisdictions and fragmentation of authority will lead to a duplication of functions and will be a wasteful and inefficient method of providing public goods and services in urban areas. Considered from this perspective, efficiency can be enhanced by eliminating overlapping jurisdictions and fragmentation of authority until all units of government are consolidated into a single unit of government for each major urban area.

These presumptions were reinforced by a further presumption that large organizations permit greater specialization within the structure of an administrative system and thus encourage increasing professionalization of the public service. Professionalization of the public service is associated with increased efficiency in the provision of public goods and services.

Adherents to this older reform tradition view the problem of coping with representation and expression of citizen preferences as one of providing means for determining the general overall "public interest" of an entire metropolitan area in contrast to local, or specialized, interests of different locales within the area. The prospects for realizing the overall public interest would be enhanced by concentrating authority in the hands of a few representative officials who would determine general policies for the entire area. Citizens would presumably benefit by being able to realize their own greater potential within the public interest of the larger community.

By seeking to realize the overall public interest of the larger urban community, those supporting consolidation presume that such a structure would be responsive to the true interests of all citizens. However, the latent problem of local specialized interests always remains as a threat. Those interests, like evil spirits, need to be suppressed if the larger public interest is to prevail. To advocates of consolidation, a system of government responsive to localized interests is the antithesis of good government. Thus, the older reform tradition is ambivalent about responsiveness as a criterion applicable to the performance of a political system. A political system should be responsive to the "true" interests of citizens as reflected in the general public interest but should be unresponsive to local, specialized interests.

The new reform tradition proposing community control turns critically upon the issue of responsiveness and challenges the presumption that only a single overall community of interest can exist in a metropolitan region. Instead these analysts presume that there are diverse communities of interest within an urban region and that neighborhood governments or community councils are necessary to the realization of these diverse interests. The community control tradition also challenges the presumption that professionalization of the public service will necessarily enhance efficiency.

Policy analysts in the public choice tradition view a system of government characterized by fragmentation of authority and overlapping jurisdictions as creating opportunities to exploit diverse economies of scale. Thus, they would expect a system of government comprised of many different and overlapping units to have the potential for being more efficient than a fully consolidated system in which only one unit of government prevailed in each urban region.

Public choice analysts recognize that spillover effects and interdependencies among local units of government can generate a competitive rivalry that may be adverse to the interests of the different communities of people organized in each local unit. But they argue that such conflicts can be resolved through the institutional facilities of overlapping governments. Interjurisdictional warfare can be avoided if ample overlap exists in a highly federalized system.

Public choice analysts further suggest that diverse communities of interest will exist in relation to many different public goods and services in any particular urban region. From this perspective a system of government composed of many different units will be more responsive to the interests of citizens than a single government for any one urban region.

These diverse contentions might be viewed as meaningless babble which presents the serious minded citizen with an impossible task of choosing among experts who offer contradictory diagnoses and prescriptions. What can reasonable people do when confronted with contradictory formulations of expert opinions? They can attempt to understand the basic concepts and arguments inherent in the different approaches and then attempt to evaluate the explanatory power of each by the degree to which it is supported by evidence. When contradictory conclusions are reached, presumably the weight of evidence will support one or another mode of analysis.

Evidence on Government Cost and Efficiency

It is difficult to determine the relative efficiency of different size governmental units for different functions. Many goods and services are not easily measurable, and thus, outputs of different size units are not easily compared. Also, it is difficult to determine citizen evaluation of goods and services not obtained in voluntary transactions. It must be remembered that producer efficiency is meaningless without reference to consumer satisfaction.

Enumerating local governments. If studies and reports based upon the older reform tradition are carefully examined, the assertions regarding fragmentation of authority, overlapping jurisdictions and duplication of functions are usually accompanied by an enumeration of the governmental jurisdictions existing within different metropolitan areas. These enumerations are accompanied by indications that many units of local government are relatively small in relation to size of population and geographical area served. Citizens in any particular area are identified as being served by several different units of government. Extreme cases of ten or more units of government serving the residents of a specific area are given as illustrations of the amount of overlap. On the basis of these observations, the following type of conclusion is reached about "the need for local government reform":

> The bewildering multiplicity of small, piecemeal, duplicative, overlapping jurisdictions cannot cope with the staggering difficulties encountered in managing urban affairs. The fiscal efforts of duplicative suburban separatism create great difficulties in provision of costly central city services benefiting the whole urbanized area. If local governments are to function effectively in metropolitan areas, they must have sufficient size and authority to plan, administer and provide for financial support to area-wide problems.[1]

Such assertions simply reiterate the basic theoretical presumptions which associate fragmentation of authority and overlapping jurisdictions with institutional failure of local governmental organization in metropolitan areas. Enumerations of local governmental units in any particular metropolitan area provide only census-type data about the number of units, population and area served. No data are provided about the costs of public services, the output of public services nor the relative efficiency with which public services are produced. Whether a single unit of government or a multiplicity of governmental jurisdictions enable citizens to cope effectively with the "staggering difficulties" encountered in the conduct of urban public affairs is left uninformed by evidence. The answer is presumed.

Similarly, the President's Commission on Law Enforcement and the Administration of Justice described the "machinery of law enforcement in this country" as "fragmented, complicated, and frequently overlapping":

> America is essentially a nation of small police forces, each operating independently within the limits of its jurisdiction. The boundaries which define and limit police operations do not hinder the movement of criminals. . . . They can and do take advantage of ancient political and geographic boundaries, which give them sanctuary from effective police activity.[2]

The President's commission enumerates the multiplicity of police departments serving the different metropolitan areas in the United

---

[1] Committee for Economic Development, *Modernizing Local Government* (New York, 1966), p. 44. Quoted with emphasis added in CED, *Reshaping Government in Metropolitan Areas* (New York, 1970), p. 16.

[2] President's Task Force on Law Enforcement and Administration of Justice, *The Challenge of Crime in a Free Society* (New York: Avon Books, 1967), p. 301.

States: 313 county forces and 4,144 municipal forces. *No reference is made to the state and federal police forces providing the same metropolitan areas with area-wide services.* The commission then goes on to recommend that "each metropolitan area and each county should take action directed toward the pooling, or consolidation, of police services through the technique that will provide the most satisfactory law enforcement service and protection at lowest cost." [3] Again, the President's commission simply presumed that consolidation will result in the "most satisfactory law enforcement service and protection at lowest cost."

Size and per capita costs. If the causal relationships assumed by the consolidation reform approach were to be supported by evidence, then we would expect (1) an increase in the size of jurisdictions and (2) a decrease in the number or multiplicity of jurisdictions to result in lower costs for the provision of public services. Can we secure evidence which gives weight to the conclusion that an increase in size of jurisdictions and a decrease in the multiplicity of jurisdictions will either improve services at a given level of expenditure or involve less cost at a given level of service?

Some very crude data can be secured on the relationships between the size of municipalities in terms of populations and the amount of per capita expenditure. A comparison of cities with different size populations with average per capita expenditures for each group is given in Table 1.

Table 1
PER CAPITA EXPENDITURES BY CITY SIZE

Population	1966-67	1970-71	Percent Increase 1966-67—1970-71
Less than 50,000	$ 96	$125	30.2%
50,000 - 99,999	161	189	17.4
100,000 - 199,999	177	235	32.8
200,000 - 299,999	160	263	64.4
300,000 - 499,999	175	270	54.3
500,000 - 999,999	233	350	50.2
Over 1,000,000	321	569	77.2
All municipalities	164	242	47.6

Source: U.S. Bureau of the Census, *City Government Finances in 1966-67* and *1970-71* (Washington, D. C.: U.S. Government Printing Office).

[3] Ibid, p. 308.

As city size increases there is a marked increase in per capita expenditures for city services. A long train of studies shows comparable results. A number of British studies have examined the relationship of municipal expenditures to city size and have concluded that major diseconomies of scale are found in large cities, especially those with populations of more than 250,000.[4] A number of recent American studies concerned with "determinants" of municipal expenditures have indicated a positive relationship between increasing city size and increasing per capita expenditures.[5] After a review of the literature on city size and per capita expenditures for police services, E. Ostrom and R. Parks report that, *"No one has reported a negative relationship between city size and per capita expenditures on police."* (Their emphasis.) [6]

Such data clearly do *not* support the contention that an increase in organizational size associated with consolidation will reduce costs. Several possible explanations might be offered for this discrepancy between expectations and evidence. One explanation would be based upon a presumption that increasing city size is associated with diseconomies of scale in which bigger units become more costly rather than less costly to run. Diseconomies of scale would be associated with disproportionately high management costs in relation to services rendered. Another explanation might be offered by assuming that increasing city size is associated with improvements in the range and quality of public services supplied by cities. Still another explanation could be based upon the fact that large cities serve nonresidents, who come into the city to work and shop, as well as city residents, and thus one should expect big cities to have higher costs for public

---

[4] C. A. Baker, "Population and Costs in Relation to City Management," *Journal of the Royal Statistics Society*, vol. 73 (December 1910), pp. 73-89. London County Council, *Comparative Municipal Statistics, 1912-1913* (London: Local Government and Statistics Department, 1915). Oxford University, *A Survey of the Social Services in the Oxford District* (London: Oxford University Press, 1938). H. S. Phillips, "Municipal Efficiency and Town Size," *Journal of the Town Planning Institute*, vol. 28 (May-June 1942), pp. 139-148.

[5] R. W. Bahl, *Metropolitan City Expenditures: A Comparative Analysis* (Lexington: University of Kentucky Press, 1969). L. R. Gabler, "Economies and Diseconomies of Scale in Urban Public Sectors," *Land Economics*, vol. 47 (May 1971), pp. 130-138. E. P. Fowler and R. L. Lineberry, "The Comparative Analysis of Urban Policy: Canada and the United States," in H. Hahn, ed. *People and Politics in Urban Society* (Beverly Hills, Calif.: Sage Publications, 1971), pp. 345-368.

[6] E. Ostrom and R. Parks, "Suburban Police Departments: Too Many and Too Small?" in Louis H. Masotte and Jeffrey K. Hadden, *Urban Affairs Annual Reviews: The Urbanization of the Suburbs*, vol. 7 (Beverly Hills, Calif.: Sage Publications, 1973), pp. 367-402.

services. Still another explanation could be that costs of government services are related to factors such as population density, which in general are higher in larger cities, and not to political organization. In summary, the simple relationship between size and per capita costs for municipal services does not tell us anything about either government efficiency or citizen satisfaction with local public service outputs.

Multiplicity of jurisdictions and per capita costs. In attempts to better understand the relationships between per capita costs and government organization, analysts have tried to identify "determinants" of municipal expenditures. Of special interest to questions of reform through consolidation is how the number of jurisdictions in metropolitan areas is related to expenditures. R. W. Bahl included the number of jurisdictions in a metropolitan area as a measure of multiplicity in a seventeen variable statistical analysis of 1960 expenditures for 198 American cities.[7] Bahl found that the number of governmental jurisdictions accounted for very little difference in per capita operating expenditures from one metropolitan area to another. What little difference he did find indicated that the larger the number of jurisdictions, the lower the per capita expenditure.

In other studies Campbell and Sacks found no consistent relationship between measures of "fragmentation" and per capita expenditures.[8] Hawkins and Dye, however, did identify a weak but statistically significant positive relationship between the number of municipalities in a Standard Metropolitan Statistical Area and police expenditures, and a negative relationship between the number of governments per 100,000 population and police expenditures.[9] Both these studies resulted in the conclusion that fragmentation did not have much effect on governmental expenditure.

Ostrom and Parks, in their analysis of the data obtained for the President's Commission on Law Enforcement and the Administration of Justice in the national criminal victimization study, included two measures of multiplicity: the number of police departments serving each metropolitan area and the number of police departments serving a metropolitan area per 100,000 population. When the first measure of multiplicity was used, a weak positive relationship was identified

---

[7] R. W. Bahl, *Metropolitan City Expenditure*, pp. 62-68.

[8] A. K. Campbell and S. Sacks, *Metropolitan America* (New York: The Free Press, 1967), p. 179.

[9] B. W. Hawkins and T. R. Dye, "Metropolitan 'Fragmentation': A Research Note," *Midwest Review of Public Administration*, vol. 4 (February 1970), p. 205.

between the number of jurisdictions and higher costs for police services. However, when multiplicity was measured by the number of police departments per 100,000 population, the evidence strongly supported the opposite conclusion: the more jurisdictions per 100,000 population, the lower are the per, capita expenditures for police services.[10]

It is difficult to relate determinants of expenditures to questions of government efficiency. Efficiency is concerned with the relationship of expenditures to levels of output and citizen satisfaction. Large expenditures and poor services are quite different than large expenditures and good services. The critical issue is whether people are getting their money's worth in services at any given level of expenditure. Studies of the determinants of expenditures do not provide satisfactory evidence on questions of efficiency.

Size and the output of public services. In Chapter 4 we indicated the results of several studies comparing matched neighborhoods (with equivalent socioeconomic characteristics of population, housing, density, et cetera) served by large central city police forces and small independent police forces. Indicators such as victimization, response time and level of follow-up were used to measure the quality of police services. Citizens served by the smaller jurisdictions consistently rated the quality of police services as equal to or better than the services provided in comparable neighborhoods served by central city police forces when compared on those indicators.

Werner Hirsch has reviewed a number of studies made by economists who have attempted to use some consistent measure of output to determine economies of scale in the public sector.[11] The conclusion to be drawn from Hirsch's efforts is that economies of scale vary among the different services supplied in the public sector. Some services are more efficiently produced by large jurisdictions; others are more efficiently produced by smaller units. Services possessing economies of scale or other characteristics making provision by large units relatively efficient include air pollution control, water supply, sewage disposal, public transportation, electric power production, hospitals and some health services. Other services such as education, police and fire services, libraries, public housing, welfare, parks and

---

[10] Ostrom and Parks, "Suburban Police Departments," p. 390.

[11] Werner Z. Hirsch, "Local Versus Areawide Urban Government Services," *National Tax Journal,* vol. 17 (December 1964). Werner Z. Hirsch, "The Supply of Urban Public Services," in Harvey S. Perloff and Lowden Wingo Jr., eds., *Issues in Urban Economics* (Baltimore: The Johns Hopkins Press, 1968).

recreation, refuse collection and street maintenance do not appear to possess declining average costs for cities with populations above 50,000 to 100,000.

The Advisory Commission on Intergovernmental Relations has, consistent with Hirsch's findings, concluded that "size does not seem to matter in cities of 25,000 to 250,000—neither economies nor diseconomies of scale were of significant number. But in cities over 250,000 population, size *does* make a difference—the law of diminishing returns sets in and there are significant *diseconomies* of scale." [12]

These conclusions regarding diseconomies of scale cast substantial doubt about the presumption that increasing size will yield decreasing average costs and/or increasing efficiency. The opposite conclusion is supported by the predominant weight of evidence: increasing size beyond a moderate level yields increasing diseconomies for many services, especially those which are highly labor intensive.

While studies attempting to identify economies of scale come closer to relating governmental size to efficiency than do studies of expenditures, they too face serious problems. The major difficulty is that these studies rely upon only crude indicators of output. This difficulty is inherent in studies of public goods and services as we emphasized in Chapter 3.

In spite of their shortcomings these studies are the best we have at the present time. They do not support the consolidation-reform diagnosis of urban problems, and indicate that our larger cities are already much too large for the efficient production of labor intensive public goods and services where person-to-person relationships have a significant effect upon the quality of services. However, they do indicate that large jurisdictions will realize economies of scale in providing capital intensive services such as water and sewerage works, hospitals, airports and other transportation facilities and services which impinge upon people over wide areas, such as air pollution control.[13]

---

[12] Advisory Commission on Intergovernmental Relations, *Size Can Make a Difference. A Closer Look* (Washington, D. C.: Advisory Commission on Intergovernmental Relations, Bulletin No. 70-8, 1970), p. 2.

[13] Other serious problems in studies of economies of scale in the public sector include: (1) There are no a priori reasons to expect public organizations where no competition exists and "owners" cannot put profits in their pocket to operate with efficient input combinations. Thus the cost functions derived from data for public firms do not possess the same internal characteristics as cost functions for private firms operating under competitive conditions, and no real conclusion on potential efficiency for different sized units can be drawn. (2) Many analysts do not specify output clearly, and they mix supply and demand variables together improperly. Thus the resulting "function" is not a cost function suitable

Professionalization. The older reform tradition places an important emphasis on professionalization, and it is hard to find recommendations for governmental change that do not include statements on the necessity of "upgrading" personnel to achieve improved performance. Higher levels of professionalization among government employees are also supposed to facilitate managing large organizations because the higher skill levels permit greater specialization, and common professional orientation increases uniformity and reliability of outputs.

Recent analyses of professional behavior vis à vis their clients in police, education and social work have raised serious questions about the beneficial consequences of professionalism.[14] In these crucial areas, critics accuse professionals of being more concerned for their own welfare than that of their clients, and of not really knowing how to improve outputs and solve problems in their own fields of expertise. Both Robert M. Fogelson and the Kerner Commission Report conclude that professionalized police forces do not necessarily lead to improved performance in terms of client satisfaction.[15] Marilyn Gittell and David Rogers are just two of many educational analysts who have concluded that teachers have neither the knowledge nor the concern to improve the educational performance of students of cultural backgrounds different from their own.[16] Richard A. Cloward, Frances Piven and Neil Gilbert are three of many analysts of social welfare programs who bring a similar indictment: professionals may lack both knowledge and concern for their clients.[17]

It is difficult to determine the reason for professional behavior which appears to be detrimental to client and citizen interests. It

---

for identifying economies of scale, but some unexplained hybrid that we do not have a solid basis for interpreting. Some of these issues are discussed in Richard A. Musgrave's "Discussion of Part III" (articles by Netzer, Hirsch, and Margolis on financing, supply and demand for public goods, respectively), in Perloff and Wingo, eds., *Issues in Urban Economics*, pp. 567-574.

[14] For a good analysis of the crisis of confidence in professionalism see Marie R. Haug and Marvin B. Sussman, "Professional Autonomy and the Revolt of the Client," *Social Problems*, vol. 17 (Fall 1969), pp. 153-161.

[15] Robert M. Fogelson, "From Resentment to Confrontation: The Police, the Negroes and the Outbreak of the 1960's Riots," *Political Science Quarterly*, vol. 83 (June 1968), pp. 217-247; *Report of the Advisory Commission on Civil Disorders* (New York: Bantam, 1968), pp. 301-305.

[16] Marilyn Gittell, "Decision-Making in the Schools: New York City, A Case Study," in Marilyn Gittell, ed., *Educating an Urban Population* (Beverly Hills, Calif.: Sage Publications, 1967), David Rogers, *110 Livingston Street* (New York: Random House, 1968).

[17] Frances Fox Piven and Richard A. Cloward, *Regulating the Poor: The Functions of Public Welfare* (New York: Pantheon, 1971), and Neil Gilbert, *Clients or Constituents: Community Action in the War on Poverty* (San Francisco: Jossey-Bass, 1970).

could be due to the loss of information and control which occurs in large-scale bureaucratic structures. The voice that citizens have in relation to official policies is exceptionally weak in large center cities. Similarly, the amount of discretion exercised by the individual professional employee is narrowly constrained by organizational policies and procedures. The professional employee may become a cog in a machine where the costs of conforming may be significantly less than the costs of innovative problem solving and attempting to modify practices in the system.

The negative aspects of professionalism may also be due, in part, to a lack of knowledge concerning client preferences, especially when clients possess significantly different socioeconomic characteristics from the professional worker. The very process of professionalization is one in which individuals are indoctrinated into a particular work ethic and way of thinking about the world that is different from that held by other persons. Thus, it may well be that the very process of professionalization makes professionals incapable of responding to and assisting citizens from different cultural backgrounds and life styles.

Innovation and productivity increases. The measurement of efficiency and responsiveness usually deals with a known environment. Crucial questions for any kind of government organization are whether or not it can make innovative and adaptive responses to changing conditions and whether incentives exist to encourage increases in efficiency over time.

The relationship of innovation to enhanced productivity was discussed in Chapter 4 where it was noted that the Rural-Metro fire company in Scottsdale undertook innovations which reduced costs by an estimated 47 percent of those expected for the same level of services from a traditionally organized fire department. In the same chapter, the question of innovation was referred to in the discussion of the report to the President's Commission on School Finance, which concluded that school system innovation was inversely related to district size and that little or no innovation could be expected from within large systems. We also noted that innovation was observed among producers supplying services to Lakewood Plan cities which use intergovernmental contracts to take advantage of economies of scale while maintaining relatively small political units to enhance the capability of citizens to express their preferences.

Other analysts of innovation and productivity among local governments have concluded that there is a basic incompatibility between innovation and administrative efforts to obtain manageability and predictability in bureaucratic behavior.[18] Innovation by its very nature introduces "unreliability" and "unpredictability" into organizational relationships. The private sector, in which outputs are easily measurable, can permit wider latitude in individual behavior and check on the results of that behavior by simply looking at output measurements or profit and loss statements. Thus, it is possible to build incentive systems which encourage innovation directed at improving output. Innovation and increasing efficiency become sought-after objectives.

In the public sector the difficulty of measuring outputs forces a management focus on employee behavior per se, and it is extremely difficult to manage behavior as organizations increase in size. Systematic study of innovation in the local government sector is only beginning, but the weight of the evidence thus far is that innovation and incentives to undertake productivity increases and to enhance efficiency are less likely to be found in large public organizations which are not subject to competitive pressures.[19]

Observations on government cost and efficiency. An examination of evidence bearing on questions of government cost and efficiency does not let us unequivocally conclude that the public choice way of thinking about urban government leads to more useful observations than the older reform tradition advocating consolidation. The evidence, however, does raise serious questions about the traditional reform position. The process of enumerating governments that traditional reformers have relied on to support their recommendations for consolidation produces no evidence on the relationship between size or multiplicity and government efficiency. Simple cost studies, studies relating the multiplicity of jurisdictions and attempts to identify economies of scale all provide evidence that either does not support, or directly contradicts, the consolidationist position. Supplementary evidence on professionalism and innovation and productivity increases in public organizations points to similar conclusions: it

---

[18] For a survey of research, see Victor Thompson, *Bureaucracy and Innovation* (University, Ala.: University of Alabama Press, 1969).

[19] For a good empirical study see Martin M. Rosner, "Administrative Controls and Innovation," *Behavioral Science*, vol. 13 (January 1968), pp. 136-143. Also see the November/December 1972 issue of the *Public Administration Review* which is devoted to the problem of productivity increases in government. Another useful source is Harry P. Hatry and Donald M. Fisk, *Improving Productivity and Productivity Measurement in Local Governments* (Washington, D. C.: The Urban Institute, 1971).

either does not support or directly contradicts recommendations for consolidation.

Judging the evidence in relation to the public choice approach is much more difficult because that approach concludes that a variety of institutional arrangements is necessary to take into account the diversity in public goods and services and the diversity in citizen preferences. The only studies undertaken to directly examine the public choice approach have been the studies of fire and police cited in Chapter 4. More explicit testing of hypotheses drawn from opposing theoretical frameworks is needed before one can unequivocally recommend the public choice approach, but it appears that sufficient evidence on the failure of the consolidationist position exists to create substantial doubt that it is a very useful framework for understanding how governmental institutions work and how those institutions might be improved.

Evidence that is relevant to different approaches to urban government can also be derived from studies that deal with problems other than size, expenditure levels and efficiency considerations. These other studies include citizen attitudes and voting behavior on reform proposals, attempts to evaluate consolidated governments and some evidence bearing directly on crucial differences in the theoretical frameworks.

Citizen Attitudes and Voting Behavior

A puzzling situation or anomaly has accompanied reform efforts to consolidate different units of local government into a single jurisdiction serving a particular metropolitan region. Voter response, when voters have been presented with a decision to approve or reject consolidation in a referendum, has been distinctly *negative.* "[W]hen given the opportunity, voters generally reject this form of local governmental reorganization."[20]

If voters were rational and if voters believed that consolidation would yield improved services at equal or less cost, voters could be expected to give overwhelming support to consolidation proposals. The contrary has been the case. In view of the negative voter response, two explanations might be offered. Voters may act irrationally in the sense of voting against their known best interest, or voters may have grounds for rejecting the belief that consolidation

---

[20] V. L. Marando and C. R. Whitley, "City-County Consolidation, An Overview of Voter Response," *Urban Affairs Quarterly,* vol. 8 (December 1972), pp. 181-203, 183.

will yield improved services at equal or less cost. Given the weight of the evidence that we have already explored, voters would appear to have grounds for rejecting consolidation proposals. However, studies of citizen attitudes and voting behavior provide interesting data for students of urban affairs to ponder in relation to alternative explanations of governmental performance.

Marando and Whitley report that the substance of a consolidation proposal will influence voter support. The more councilmen and more separately elected administrative officials provided for in the proposal, the higher the voter support for a consolidation proposal will be.[21] Voters apparently view a constitutional arrangement under which only a few policy making officials are elected and a single chief executive can control a highly integrated administrative command structure as having high potential costs. This conclusion is consistent with the cost calculus developed by James Buchanan and Gordon Tullock in their theory of constitutional choice. They expect potential deprivation costs to be relatively high with fewer elected officials.[22]

Marando and Whitley also report that the strong centers of potential voter opposition are "politically appeased" in consolidation proposals by excluding small incorporated municipalities. Excluding these municipalities reduces voter opposition by reducing in advance the number of voters opposed to consolidation.[23]

The number of special districts existing in an area proposing consolidation is negatively related to voter support for consolidation. Marando and Whitley suggest that special districts provide most of the services which urbanites desire and the existence of special districts is viewed as meeting the needs for which consolidation is being proposed.[24]

In a study of voter attitudes conducted after the election approving consolidation of Nashville and Davidson County, Tennessee, B. W. Hawkins found a very strong relationship between those who were dissatisfied with existing services and their vote in support of consolidation.[25] Nearly two-thirds of those who were dissatisfied with existing services and anticipated higher costs voted in support of consolidation. On the other hand, those who were satisfied with services and anticipated higher costs voted nearly three to one

---

[21] Ibid., p. 191.
[22] James M. Buchanan and Gordon Tullock, *The Calculus of Consent* (Ann Arbor: University of Michigan Press, 1962), pp. 63-84.
[23] Marando and Whitley, "City-County Consolidation," p. 192.
[24] Ibid., p. 193.
[25] B. W. Hawkins, "Public Opinion and Metropolitan Consolidation in Nashville," *Journal of Politics*, vol. 28 (May 1966), pp. 408-418.

against consolidation. Those who were satisfied with services and did not anticipate higher costs, and those who were dissatisfied with services and did not anticipate higher costs voted overwhelmingly in favor of consolidation.

It appears that voters in Nashville-Davidson County used a relatively conscious calculus in making their decisions to vote for or against consolidation. Their basic difficulty centered in the problem of attaching a realistic price tag to the alternatives before them. Advocates of consolidation promised improved services supplied more economically. A survey done by R. E. McArthur three years after consolidation of Nashville-Davidson County indicated that 58.1 percent of the citizens considered services to be about the same as before consolidation.[26] Sixty percent of the respondents considered their taxes too high for the services received. During the first year of consolidation, tax rates in the consolidated General Services District increased by 34.1 percent over the 1962-63 county tax rate. Whether voters had accurately assessed the price tag attached to the consolidation proposal in Nashville-Davidson County is doubtful.

These studies of citizen attitudes and voting behavior suggest that voters have been rationally cautious in resisting consolidation proposals. When voter assessments are added to evidence regarding diseconomies of scale, the cumulative weight of the evidence is rather strongly against those who advocate consolidation as a means for "modernizing" local government and improving the quality of urban life.

Studies of Reforms

While voters have rejected most consolidation efforts in the United States, a few partial consolidations have been implemented, most notably Miami-Dade County, Florida, Nashville-Davidson County, Tennessee, Jacksonville-Duvall County, Florida, and recently Indianapolis-Marion County, Indiana. Several Canadian urban areas have also been partially consolidated, the most prominent of which is Toronto.

A large number of articles and books have been published describing consolidations and the benefits expected to flow from them. For the most part, however, little empirical evidence has been developed to determine whether or not metropolitan consolidation produces

---

[26] R. E. McArthur, *Impact of City-County Consolidation of the Rural-Urban Fringe: Nashville-Davidson County, Tenn.*, Agricultural Economic Report No. 206, Economic Research Service, U.S. Department of Agriculture (Washington, D. C.: Government Printing Office, 1971), p. 20.

the consequences which proponents expect. Stephen Erie, John Kirlin and Francine Rabinowitz have surveyed various writing on consolidated metropolitan governments to determine what the impact has been.[27] They claim only to summarize what other writers have found; they do not critically evaluate the studies they summarize. They made the following findings:

(1) Professionals have increased their impact on policy making. (This is in keeping with metropolitan reform expectations, but as we have noted earlier it need not enhance citizens' satisfaction with public goods and services.)

(2) Few scale economies have been identified except for large metropolitan districts. (This is contrary to reform expectations but in keeping with empirical studies cited earlier.)

(3) In the short run, access by minorities is guaranteed by the apportionment of representatives, but in the long run it may well be diluted.

(4) Service levels increased as did fiscal burdens and costs. (Only if services increased relative to costs are reform expectations met.)

(5) The emphasis is on tangible, physical goods, not social problems or social services. (This is in keeping with observations that person-to-person services are the most difficult to manage in large-scale organizations.)

(6) There is no immediate short-term impact on the redistribution of power or wealth.

(7) Citizen understandings and attitudes toward local and area-wide political processes remain largely unchanged.[28]

An examination of conclusions on consolidations, especially when the potential weaknesses of the studies are recognized, does not provide much evidence regarding the usefulness of alternative ways of thinking about urban government. Reform predictions are borne out with regard to professionalism, but as we previously noted this need not enhance citizen satisfaction with public goods and services. The lack of economies of scale is contrary to reform predictions. Without supplementary information, the other conclusions do not bear directly

---

[27] Stephen P. Erie, John J. Kirlin and Francine F. Rabinowitz, "Can Something Be Done? Propositions on the Performance of Metropolitan Institutions," in Lowdon Wingo, ed., *Reform of Metropolitan Governments* (Baltimore: The Johns Hopkins Press, 1972), pp. 7-41.

[28] Ibid., pp. 36-37.

on the question of which approach to understanding urban government is more useful.

Even less is known about decentralizing a big system than is known about the impact of consolidation. The studies of police departments in Chicago, Indianapolis and Grand Rapids indicate that relatively small departments can provide as high a level of service at equal or less cost than big departments. Hallman provides the following observation on decentralization and the role of smaller units within New York City:

> The network of community corporations in New York City is not remarkably efficient. There is much slippage in the system, a lot of wheel spinning, and the end product of new opportunities and better services for the poor people seems to be relatively small in proportion to expenditures and efforts made. Yet the present arrangement is accomplishing more in concrete program results than the more centralized system of municipal control that previously existed.[29]

It is impossible, however, to draw firm conclusions on the basis of the evidence presently available.

Evidence Bearing on Crucial Theoretical Differences

Because assumptions are extreme abstractions of reality, it is not possible to test them directly.[30] Tests of different assumptions must ultimately be related to how well they help one predict, diagnose and prescribe solutions to problems. However, given the lack of evidence supporting consolidation, it is useful to examine more closely four crucial differences between the older reform tradition and the public choice approach to understanding urban government. To as great an extent as possible, empirical evidence relating to predictions derived from the assumptions will be cited.

The behavioral assumption: Are public officials benevolent or self-interested? According to traditional American constitutional theory, the government of the United States was organized as a system of checks and balances, each branch constrained by its counterparts, so that citizens would not be dependent upon the benevolence of a single

---

[29] Howard W. Hallman, *Neighborhood Control of Public Programs* (New York: Praeger, 1970), p. 206.

[30] For a discussion of the problems of testing assumptions, see Milton Friedman, "The Methodology of Positive Economics," in *Essays on Positive Economics* (Chicago: University of Chicago Press, 1953).

set of public officials with all the reins of power in its grasp. The concept that the authority of government should be concentrated in the hands of a few elected officials so that those officials can exercise the full responsibility of government presumes that such officials will act with substantial benevolence in their devotion to the public interest. Can such a presumption stand critical scrutiny?

The creation of independent regulatory commissions depends upon conditions where the members are supposed to act benevolently to protect public interests during their term of office. There have been many studies of regulatory commissions, and the conclusions are that commissioners quickly adopt the perspective of the industry they are supposed to regulate, proceeding to serve as protectors of that industry, often promoting policies which are of doubtful public interest.[31] At least in the case of regulatory commissions, the assumptions of benevolence do not appear to aid in *predicting* operational behavior. The studies on professionalization cited earlier suggest that the assumption of benevolence is not useful for deriving conclusions that will accurately predict behavioral patterns.

One reason the usefulness of the assumptions of benevolence and self-interest are difficult to test in the American public economy is that many institutions are structured so that action under either motivation would be the same. For example, an elected official who wants to be reelected is likely to find it in his self-interest to take his constituents' interests into account in his public actions. However, there are sufficient examples of corruption and neglect of constituent interests by public officials to at least consider the assumption that public officials, like private businessmen or consumers, may find it to be in their own self-interest to act against the public interest.[32] Only when institutions are structured so that officials are, in their own self-interest, led to search out solutions which will be of public benefit can we have confidence in the essential structure of urban government.

Knowledge. The reform tradition recommending consolidation presumes that large-scale organizations can obtain, process and use large quantities of information regarding public needs, availability of resources, techniques of efficient production and efficient and equitable delivery of services to citizens. Just how much information can be

---

[31] Good analysis of the problems of regulatory commissions are contained in Roger G. Noll, *Reforming Regulation* (Washington: The Brookings Institution, 1971) and Louis M. Kohlmier, Jr., *The Regulators: Watchdog Agencies and the Public Interest* (New York: Harper and Row, 1969).

[32] Gordon S. Black, "A Theory of Political Ambition," *American Political Science Review*, vol. 66 (1972), pp. 144-159.

obtained, processed and collected for use by a single decision maker or small group of decision makers within a single organization? There is considerable evidence that large hierarchies are not dependable mechanisms for accumulating information, digesting it and passing it to relevant decision makers.[33] The information loss and distortion occurring at each level of organization are simply too great. Large organizations exist so that subordinates can make decisions independently and so that management can assess the consequences of their decisions in terms of outputs or profit and loss statements. The problem with public bureaucracies is compounded because there are no profit and loss statements, goods are usually not sold and outputs themselves are extremely difficult to measure.

There is a large body of economic planning and business management literature concerned with the difficulty of accumulating and evaluating information.[34] On the basis of this literature and studies of the information processing capacity of bureaucracies, it would appear that the assumption that a high level of knowledge can be accumulated at a single decision-point in a complex environment is not a useful one for predictive purposes. It would appear much more reasonable to begin with the assumption that knowledge for decision making is difficult and costly to acquire and that central decision makers will be greatly subject to error.

Citizen preferences: heterogeneous or homogeneous. The reform tradition recommending consolidation presumes that citizens' preferences are similar and that uniform levels of all public goods and services should be provided in metropolitan areas. What if large bureaucracies could produce uniform levels of services innovatively, at low cost and in relation to uniform preferences among the population? If such were the case, advantages would accrue from large-scale organizations. Many aspects of government, especially with reference to the operation of the federal and state governments, relate to such conditions. Uniformities in the design and layout of interstate highways and in the rules applicable to driving motor vehicles, for example, have obvious advantages for everyone who uses those highways.

---

[33] An empirical analysis of information problems in organizations is presented in Oliver Williamson, "Hierarchical Control and Optimum Firm Size," *Journal of Political Economy*, vol. 75 (April 1967), pp. 123-138. An excellent discussion of information difficulties is presented in Gordon Tullock's *The Politics of Bureaucracy* (Washington, D. C.: Public Affairs Press, 1965).

[34] See the last two chapers in James G. March and Herbert A. Simon, *Organizations* (New York: John Wiley and Sons, 1958), for a discussion of the cognitive limits of rationality and of planning and innovation in organizations.

Citizens appear to have different preferences for many public goods and services, just as they have different preferences for private goods and services. At one time it was assumed that after sufficient time in the melting pot, all citizens' preferences and life styles would be similar. This view has been challenged.[35] Diverse preferences for public services complicate problems of public sector organization. One cannot assume that there is one best way to meet diverse preferences for different public goods and services. Much more attention needs to be paid to how citizens indicate their preferences, and how those preferences can be met.

Diversity of public goods and services. The consolidation approach presumes that public goods and services are sufficiently similar that they all can be provided most efficiently by the same organization. This presumption has been modified by those advocating a two-tier system.

Goods and services commonly thought of as public include education, police and fire services, the provision of parks and recreation programs, water and sewer services, provision of streets, sidewalks and street lighting, traffic control, public transportation, licensing and inspecting restaurants, food stores, elevators, food processing plants, regulating air and water pollution, providing for solid waste disposal, maintaining animal control and pound facilities, operating an office to promote tourism or industrial development, collecting taxes and operating airports and seaports. Individual contract cities in California have as many as forty-nine separate contracts with county governments for different goods and services, and these are supplemented with other contracts with private producers and memberships in special districts.

Not only are local governments responsible for a diverse set of activities, but when one looks in detail at each activity, one discovers differences in economies of scale and organizational requirements. For example, police foot patrol is undertaken on a different level of organization than radio dispatching, criminal investigation, crime laboratory analysis, the provision of jails, the control of organized crime, the international pursuit of criminals and narcotics control and

---

[35] For surveys see Michael Parenti, "Ethnic Politics and the Persistence of Ethnic Identification," *American Political Science Review*, vol. 61 (September 1967), pp. 717-726, and Andrew M. Greeley, *Why Can't They Be Like Us: America's White Ethnic Groups* (New York: Dutton, 1971). For a good empirical study of a single city see Norman J. Johnson and Peggy R. Sanday, "Subcultural Variations in an Urban Poor Population," *American Anthropologist*, vol. 73 (February 1971), pp. 123-143.

the training of different kinds of policemen from community relations specialists to demolition experts. The diversity among public activities with respect to economies of scale, boundaries for inclusion under a single organization or by agreements among different organizations, the measurability of outputs, and the problem of standardization versus the need for differentiation to meet diverse citizen preferences all point to potential problems in structuring different organizational arrangements. We do not believe it can be *assumed* that a simple consolidated system or even a two-tier system of government is adequate for citizens to articulate their preferences and for agencies to produce the variety of public services needed by urban residents. Coordination, where needed, is possible through a variety of institutional arrangements and contractual agreements.

Conclusions

In this chapter we have analyzed empirical evidence that permits us to weigh the relative usefulness of alternative ways of thinking about urban government. We believe the review of evidence supports three major conclusions: First, there is *not* a high level of empirical evidence at hand to clarify what approach offers the best explanation of how governmental institutions work. Second, what evidence does exist either does not support or directly contradicts the conclusions and recommendations of the traditional reform approach. And third, recent studies provide some evidence that the public choice approach, which focuses on the diversity of individual preferences and the diverse nature of public goods and services, may be useful for understanding problems and recommending improvements in urban government.

These studies also provide support for the advocates of community control and neighborhood government. However, concern over community control and neighborhood government focuses upon only a selective aspect of urban government. The basic issue that we confront in seeking to understand urban government is what concepts and theoretical framework will help us to explain what has occurred, diagnose what has gone wrong and explore alternative options that may be available to us. The two-tier solution is a compromise between contending formulations, but we are left with a puzzle as to why the magic number two affords us with the appropriate solution. If we include federal and state agencies as producers of area-wide services in each metropolitan area, do we not have at least a four-tier arrangement if a two-tier metropolitan government is adopted? We are still confronted with a task of deciding what concepts and conceptual apparatus will enable us to understand urban government. Once this is worked out, we should be able to derive solutions, whether or not those solutions include neighborhood governments, "two-tierness," or "four-tierness."

The lack of evidence about the performance of different systems of urban government is due in large part to the unquestioning acceptance of presumptions and conclusions of the traditional reform approach which have dominated the analysis of urban government during the last century. It has only been the obvious failures within big city governments and criticisms raised by reformers recommending decentralization that has led to a serious questioning of both the diagnosis and prescriptions offered by the traditional analysts favoring consolidation. We believe that a review of evidence directly related to the causal inferences inherent in the traditional reform approach indicates severe limitations in that approach.

Because the public choice approach focuses on diversity of both individual preferences and the nature of public goods and services, it recommends no single institutional structure for urban government. The implication of this approach is that an industry or public economy orientation, from which government operations are considered as those of diverse agencies producing different bundles of public goods and services, may be more useful for analyzing urban government than an approach which presumes that a fully integrated monopoly will be best able to produce all public goods and services equally well. The studies undertaken specifically to test the public choice approach—the study of the Rural-Metro fire company in Scottsdale, and the police performance studies in Indianapolis, Grand Rapids and Chicago—provide strong evidence, albeit on a limited scale, of the usefulness of this approach to understanding urban government.

There is no question that much more evidence must be generated before conflicts among alternative approaches to the understanding of urban government will be resolved. In the meantime scholars, citizens and public officials should be constantly aware of the serious inadequacies of traditional approaches to the diagnosis and prescription of solutions to urban problems. We should all be prepared to ask whether our conclusions are supported by evidence. Workable solutions must be able to stand the test of experience. There is no perfect society, and all forms of organization have their price. The problem of choice is always one of assessing benefits and costs and of choosing the alternatives that offer the best prospects for advancing human welfare.

7

AN AGENDA FOR THE FUTURE

Two conclusions follow from the analysis presented in this monograph. First, sufficient evidence exists to cast profound doubts upon reform proposals to improve urban governance by the consolidation of all units of government into a single unit of government for each metropolitan area. Implementation of such proposals will probably make matters worse rather than better. Second, we need to experiment with other approaches to develop better evidence to test the usefulness of alternative ways of thinking about urban government. An approach which begins with recognition of a diversity in citizen preferences and a diversity in the nature of public goods and services is likely to be a more useful approach.

The challenges being presented by the advocates of community control and the new perspectives being provided by the public choice analysts call for serious reexamination of the diagnoses and prescriptions for urban problems currently in use. An enumeration of the number of jurisdictions together with a pointing out of the amount of overlap among jurisdictions serving a metropolitan area is not evidence that fragmentation of authority and overlapping jurisdictions are inefficient. Multiple jurisdictions, like many firms in an industry, may improve efficiency and provide higher levels of satisfaction to consumers.

The logic inherent in the design of the American political system is based upon a presumption that overlapping jurisdictions will give citizens access to multiple sets of officials to tend to their interests. That logic also presumes that authority must be divided or fragmented if those who exercise governmental prerogatives are to be held accountable for their actions. It may well be that the most critical problems of urban government have derived from excessive efforts to simplify political structures. Citizens in big cities no longer have easy access to a diversified system of government that is responsive to the many communities of interest existing in such large jurisdictions.

Fragmentation of authority does increase levels of visible conflict. But visible conflict may bring out information, clarify issues and encourage a search for mutually agreeable solutions. These potentials must be contrasted with an anticipation that highly integrated command structures may repress information, produce mistakes and result in substantial discrepancy between promise and performance. Organizing the public sector so that citizen preferences for a diverse range of public goods and services are efficiently met is a difficult task. Simple solutions are unlikely to suffice.

We anticipate that the study of urban problems during the closing decades of the twentieth century will focus on a new range of issues quite different from those stressed by the reform tradition proposing consolidation during the past half-century and with a broader focus than that stressed by the reformers advocating decentralization and community control.

We have selected eight items which we believe deserve priority for understanding and improving urban governments:

(1) *Neighborhood government.* Neighborhood government can be viewed as any small-scale effort of groups of neighbors to tend their common interests in a regular and orderly way. Neighborhood governments are crucial to resolving problems within big cities.

(2) *Multi-organizational structures.* We need to develop new ways for understanding intergovernmental relationships as being systematically related to improved productivity in the public sector in much the same way that markets provide for the organization of diverse private sector activities.

(3) *Public service contracting.* The potentials for improving governmental efficiency by contracting with private firms or other governmental units indicate this area should receive more careful consideration.

(4) *User charges, fiscal relations and income redistribution.* Improving equity and efficiency in complex governmental systems requires careful attention to revenue sources, taxation, fiscal transfers and income redistribution.

(5) *The legal architecture of complex structures.* State constitutions and legislation provide the framework within which citizens

form local political organizations. That framework further delineates conditions under which intergovernmental agreements and contracts can be made and enforced.

(6) Patterns of bureaucratic behavior. We have assumed for too long that bureaucracies are rational, efficient, cost-free patterns of organization. Such assumptions do not stand careful scrutiny; we need a much better understanding of both the potential costs and potential benefits associated with large-scale public bureaucracies.

(7) Relations among public officials, professionals and their citizen-clients. The relationship of officials and professionals to citizens can easily become a master-servant relationship unless citizens have ways and means for holding officials and professional civil servants accountable to citizen interests.

(8) New research strategies. We need to understand how ideas shape actions so that theoretical presumptions come under critical scrutiny more often than has occurred in the past.

Let us look more closely at each of these items.

Neighborhood Governments

The urban crisis has reached its most critical proportions in big cities, not in suburbia. Instead of assuming that fragmentation of authority and overlapping jurisdictions are the source of the contemporary urban crisis, we urge that the opposite proposition be entertained as a serious hypothesis—that the absence of fragmented authority and multiple jurisdictions within large central cities is the principal source of institutional failure in urban government. The absence of neighborhood governments makes it difficult for residents of urban neighborhoods to organize so that common problems can be handled in routine ways.

Residents in many big cities have undertaken extensive efforts to organize voluntary neighborhood associations to deal with neighborhood problems. However, we can expect such efforts to involve very high costs in time and effort and to be plagued by holdouts or free riders. Some people will be unwilling to bear their share of the effort and the existence of voluntary neighborhood associations will be plagued with instability. People will organize for action in extreme exigencies but purely voluntary effort will be abandoned as conditions ameliorate. If problems require routine, continuing attention, provision will need to be made for the exercise of some governmental authority. Governmental organization is also useful if voluntarism is to be supported on a regular basis.

Suburbanites draw both upon the voluntary services of community residents and the services of professional employees. Volunteers assist in the provision of fire services. Mothers serve as "helping hands" and "block mothers," providing for the security of children on neighborhood streets. Volunteers serve as teaching aides and as hospital aides. But public support for such efforts is necessary if optimal advantage is to be taken of the willingness of citizens to perform voluntary community services.

When legislation was proposed for the consolidation of the City of Indianapolis and Marion County, Indiana, into a single unit of government called UNIGOV, State Representative E. H. Lamkin (Republican, Marion County) also proposed the creation of a system of neighborhood governments which he called MINIGOV.[1] His purpose was to make a system of government available to residents of center-city neighborhoods that would serve their interests in much the same way that small municipalities have served suburban communities. Lamkin's proposal, together with Altshuler's *Community Control* and Kotler's *Neighborhood Government* points to the importance of giving serious attention to the organization of minigovernments among neighborhoods in large urban areas. Such patterns of organization may take a variety of different forms. Consideration of the appropriate forms needs to be grounded in the theory of constitutional choice which has provided the legal foundation for the organization of American society. Thomas Jefferson's concern for the organization of small elementary ward republics is in the same vein as Lamkin's concern for minigovernments.[2] Neighborhood governments have an important place on the agenda of those who are concerned about the future government of urban areas.

Multi-Organizational Structures

The government of urban areas is not confined and limited to the activities of local units of government. Many large-scale, area-wide services are supplied by state and federal agencies. Local units of

---

[1] Lamkin's proposal is presented in Indianapolis Department of Metropolitan Development, "Preliminary Communities Plan," mimeographed, December 6, 1972.

[2] Hannah Arendt, *On Revolution*, Compass Book edition (New York: The Viking Press, 1963). In the concluding chapter Arendt considers Jefferson's concern for small elemental republics for maintaining a democratic society.

government provide for elementary and secondary education, community colleges, and in a limited number of cases, municipal universities. However, states normally operate most universities and professional and graduate schools providing public higher educational services in major urban areas. As we indicated in Chapter 5, state and federal police agencies provide area-wide police services in all major metropolitan areas, and state highway departments usually construct and maintain the major highways carrying the bulk of area-wide traffic. In other words, urban public services *are* provided by diverse agencies operating at different levels of government, ranging from small neighborhood units to large federal agencies. Services are supplied by different agencies and their joint efforts need to be viewed from a multi-organizational perspective.

Where multi-organizational arrangements exist, students concerned with understanding and organizing complex systems will need to examine patterns of interaction. How, for example, are patterns of cooperation facilitated? Rather than assuming that units of government in the American federal system behave like Balkan states are imagined to behave, perhaps we should begin to inquire about the patterns of cooperation that are likely to exist. Constrained rivalry can create competitive pressures in the public sector, giving public agencies incentives to innovate, increase productive efficiency and be more sensitive to the interests of their citizen-clients.

Cooperation can deteriorate into collusion among producers occupying potential monopoly positions. As a consequence, the availability of different administrative, judicial and legislative remedies to citizens who can be adversely affected by such collusion is an essential condition for maintaining the openness and vitality of multi-organizational structures in the joint provision of a mix of different public services.

Independence among agencies in turn implies that different agencies are free to respond to different communities of interest. Snow removal, for example, is a problem in many metropolitan areas. Clearing snow on major thoroughfares should unquestionably have a high priority. But does this priority imply that neighborhood residents should be foreclosed from arranging for snow removal as a public service to be provided for neighborhood streets? Some have argued that "two different snow removal and street maintenance systems for adjoining streets—the main arterial streets being in Metro's domain—do not seem to reflect the height of efficiency." [3]

---

[3] Melvin A. Mogulof, *Five Metropolitan Governments* (Washington, D. C.: The Urban Institute, n.d.), p. 57.

From a public choice perspective the minimal condition for meeting the criterion of efficiency would require that the benefits from the "duplicative" service of removing snow from neighborhood streets exceed the costs to neighborhood residents.

Patterns of cooperation and independence of action will be accompanied by conflicts where the actions of one agency in a multi-organizational system cause harm to others. Various institutional facilities may be available for resolving problems of interagency conflict including courts of law, legislatures, regulatory agencies, professional associations and the "good offices" of informal inter-mediaries. All of these mechanisms form a part of the system of governing relationships in a multi-organizational system.

The whole area of intergovernmental relations needs to be approached from new perspectives and new concepts. Intergovernmental relations are often viewed as the source of inconveniences which would go away if consolidation efforts were fully successful. Instead we suggest that the aggregate efforts of local, state and federal agencies in any particular metropolitan area should be viewed as a public economy. The different agencies which supply *similar services* to the same clientele can then be viewed as so many public firms in a public service industry. The public economy in each metropolitan area will be composed of a variety of public service industries including the education industry, the police industry, the water industry, the health services industry and so on. In this way different agencies can be viewed as being parts of multi-organizational systems.

The work of economists concerned with industrial organization provides the rudimentary methodology for understanding the complexities associated with multi-organizational structures.[4] Different industry and public economy structures, ranging from highly integrated monopolies to highly fragmented systems, can be compared to determine the relative efficiency and responsiveness of the different types of structures. The extension of this mode of analysis to inter-agency relationships in the public sector has only begun.[5]

---

[4] See, for example, Joe S. Bain, *Industrial Organization* (New York: John Wiley and Sons, Inc., 1959).

[5] Joe S. Bain, Richard Caves and Julius Margolis, *Northern California's Water Industry: The Comparative Efficiency of Public Enterprise in Developing a Scarce Natural Resource* (Baltimore: The Johns Hopkins Press, 1966), and Vincent Ostrom, *Institutional Arrangements for Water Resource Development—With Special Reference to the California Water Industry*, PB 207 314 (Springfield, Virginia: National Technical Information Service, 1971).

Contracting for the Provision of Municipal Goods and Services

Local government contracting with other governments or private firms appears to offer significant potential for improving efficiency in the production of municipal services—as indicated by Scottsdale's contract with the Rural-Metro fire company and the development of the Lakewood Plan in California. Three benefits appear to accrue from contracting. First, the process of contracting forces development of better information on both costs and outputs. This permits the purchasing unit to specify its preferences, by weighing costs against benefits, and the producing unit to manage its operations better. Second, contracting permits the purchaser to seek alternative suppliers or produce for itself. This introduces a competitive element which exerts pressure on the producer to try to be more efficient in order to keep his business. And third, contracting permits producers and political units buying services to be organized with reference to different geographical boundaries.

The government unit buying services may be smaller in area than the producer when significant economies of scale exist on the production side. In providing the service a unit of government need only have powers to tax, to contract with vendors and to monitor performance. Other circumstances may exist where smaller units are the most efficient producers of a public service, yet the benefits may affect a much larger community of users. In that case fiscal transfers from the large unit to smaller units would be a rational strategy to assure an appropriate mix of a public good or service to satisfy the demands of the larger community of users. For example, our nation of highway users gains an advantage when the U.S. Department of Transportation buys highway service from state highway departments through the interstate freeway program.

We anticipate that contracting for services will be important to neighborhood governments, many of which will be relatively small and may not desire to produce all of their own services. They could contract for neighborhood services with the larger city, the county, a private firm or an adjacent community, wherever they could get the most efficient package of the public goods and services they desire.

We also anticipate that the opportunity to sell services to governments will encourage private firms to enter into competition in the production of some local government services. This competition would stimulate improvement among the local government agencies that chose to produce their own services.

Whether production is private, contracted with another government, or produced by the unit itself, citizen-consumers should be the ultimate beneficiaries. Careful attention will need to be given to arrangements for monitoring the performance of contract services. Collusion can replace competition and collusive cartels will tend to behave like monopolists.

User Charges, Fiscal Relations and Income Redistribution

Quid pro quo (a something-for-something exchange) fiscal relationships are extremely important in complex governmental systems composed of multiple jurisdictions. The consolidation-reform tradition has advocated that all revenues go into a single general fund to be allocated by the chief executive and a small council of central policy makers. Under this arrangement, well-organized interest groups have incentives to lobby for their own special program—for which all taxpayers pay. The net result is special programs for highly influential groups and high taxes for everyone.

For a complex system to possess self-regulating tendencies, quid pro quo relations should be built in wherever possible unless the service is specifically to achieve income redistribution. Quid pro quo transactions force beneficiaries to indicate that they value services at least as much as these services cost. There is no reason, for example, why private airplane owners and air passengers should not pay for airport facilities or why water users should be subsidized by general taxpayers. Likewise, neighborhoods which desire improved garbage pickup, street sweeping or snow removal should be able to organize to obtain that extra service *and pay for it.*

Considerable research has been devoted to user charges such as utility fees or transit fares which require individuals to pay for benefits they receive.[6] Some experience also exists with groups of users paying for benefits, as with special assessment districts for street lighting, the use of gasoline and automobile excise taxes to pay for highway facilities and the use of hunting and fishing license fees to pay for game management and fish hatchery operations. In such cases, a use tax has much the same effect as a user charge. Much more attention, however, needs to be devoted to user charge and use tax systems and the design of other institutional arrangements so that groups of beneficiaries can pay for the public benefits they

---

[6] Selma Mushkin, ed., *Public Prices for Public Products* (Washington, D. C.: The Urban Institute, 1972).

receive. Unless citizens pay for benefits received, they will demand quantities where costs to others exceed benefits to themselves. A political system can, under this circumstance, become an instrument for raiding the treasury and public funds will be treated as relatively free goods.

In addition to consideration of quid pro quo fiscal relations, concern needs to be given to the use of general taxes, such as income and sales taxes, by local governments, especially if community governments were to possess such taxing power. Many local governments already use sales and income taxes, so experience exists for analyses. It may well be that an advantage can be gained when general taxes are subject to joint administration and larger taxing jurisdictions share taxes with smaller units. Careful attention needs to be paid to mixing the use of general taxation with use taxes and user charges to obtain the benefits of both simultaneously. Consideration to this problem appears especially important if viable neighborhood governments are to be created.

Problems of poverty and income redistribution, for example, cannot be treated as a purely local matter. Labor is highly mobile. Business firms compete in regional, national and international markets. National economic regulation to maintain high levels of employment has been a national policy for several decades. No one would seriously propose that economic regulation of market forces is a purely local problem. Similarly, no one can seriously contend that the deprivations imposed by inflation upon elements in the population who do not share in rapidly rising profits or wages can be met by a redistribution of income among local property tax payers. Any significant redistribution of income will depend upon an essential national component.

Understanding the Legal Architecture
of Complex Governmental Systems

The observation has been made that "in proportion as government is free, it must be complicated. Simplicity belongs to those only where one will govern all . . . , where law is not a science but a mandate to be followed and not to be discussed."[7] The revolutionary innovation introduced into the American system of government nearly two centuries ago was the concept that a government could be de-

---

[7] Quoted by Alexander Bickel in a review of Gerald T. Dunne, *Justice Storey and the Rise of the Supreme Court*, in *The New York Times Book Review*, May 30, 1971, p. 3.

signed and established where those who govern would themselves be subject to the rule of law. Many classical political theorists had argued that this concept was a logical impossibility, that law is established and enforced by government and thus government is above the law and cannot itself be held accountable to law.

Simple governments cannot themselves be subject to the limitations and rules of law. In such a system, law indeed is a "mandate to be followed and not to be discussed." The prosperity of a simple commonwealth depends upon law abiding citizens who obey and do not challenge the commands of officials.

By contrast, the basic design of the American political system necessarily involves a complex structure of legal and political relationships. Provisions of constitutional law which limit the authority of officials must exist apart from the provisions of ordinary law enacted by officials. The separation of constitutional law from ordinary law can be sustained only so long as processes of constitutional decision making exist apart from processes of governmental law making.

If provisions of constitutional law are to be enforced against governmental officials, then governmental authority must be subject to limits. Limits can be effective only if authority is distributed among different sets of governmental officials. Thus, constitutional law can be enforced *only* where some form of separation of powers or fragmentation of authority is built into a system of government.

If people are to participate in and simultaneously tend to diverse communities of interest, they require access to diverse sets of officials in a system of concurrent governments with overlapping jurisdictions. The federalist principle implies that overlapping jurisdictions will exist and that the republican principles of self-government will exist in *all* units of government. An effective system of constitutional law can only be maintained in a complexly structured legal and political system.

Questions of constitutional law may appear to be beyond the usual range of considerations for organizing urban government. However, provisions of state constitutional or statutory law are crucial to the opportunity of citizens to undertake cooperative actions for mutual benefit. The conditions, which must be met to create a municipal corporation, a neighborhood government or a special district to deal with a particular problem the boundaries of which differ from those of other governmental units, determine whether or not a community of people can use the governmental system to resolve their problems. Constitutional law and the law of municipal corporations establish the conditions for public entrepreneurship in the same way that the ordinary law of property and contracts establish the conditions for private entrepreneurship.[8] While states differ in their provisions for local action, most states permit citizens in unincorporated areas to utilize a variety of collective instrumentalities to resolve common problems. It is not in the suburbs and rural areas where the greatest problems exist, however, but within the large central cities where only the simplest political structure is available. State constitutions and state legislatures do not provide citizens in large central cities with authority to create smaller governmental units to resolve common problems. Only if citizens have legislative or constitutional authority to develop smaller units of government within center city neighborhoods, can we expect them to acquire the capability for solving small-scale neighborhood problems.

The law of municipal corporations and local public instrumentalities needs serious reconsideration. "Dillon's rule"—a narrow construction of municipal powers as being derived from an expressed delegation of authority by the state legislature[9]—has long since ceased to be the basic principle in the law of municipal corporations in states such as California, where principles of home rule have had constitutional standing for nearly a century. Doctrines of sovereign prerogative and sovereign immunity which presume that duly constituted authorities can do no legal wrong when acting in a governmental capacity are rapidly losing their standing as fundamental legal principles.

Contract systems depend upon legal independence under general rules of law. Bargaining implies a capacity to maintain an arm's length relationship, not one of strict subordination. Yet a lawful society always presumes that independence will be constrained by general rules. The place of discretions and constraint involves a delicate issue in the law of intergovernmental relationships.

Problems also exist in the conceptualization of public properties and the lawful claims individuals can assert in relation to public properties. The public interest is not satisfactorily resolved by vesting exclusive authority over public properties in some specified public authority. That authority is a trust on behalf of a larger community

---

[8] Mark Sproule-Jones, "Strategic Tensions in the Scale of Political Analysis," *British Journal of Political Science*, vol. 1 (1972), pp. 173-191.

[9] Anwar Syed, *The Political Theory of American Local Government* (New York: Random House, 1966), pp. 53-54.

of interests and the beneficiaries of that trust should be entitled to an accounting for performance in the discharge of that trust.[10]

The consolidation-reform tradition has continually recommended that state constitutions and state legislation be modified to *prevent* citizens from creating new political units. The public choice analysis indicates that restrictions on the creation of new political units may have contributed significantly to the problems within big cities and that if such prohibitions were extended to suburban and rural areas, citizen satisfaction with public sector performance may well decline rather than improve. Again we have competing explanations and predictions which require more empirical investigation, and which should be the subject of serious research efforts.

In any case, the answers are likely to be much more complex than is indicated by traditional reform positions. Improvements in urban government depend upon a knowledge of the consequences likely to follow from different structural conditions. Understanding the legal architecture of complex systems is an essential item on an agenda for the future.

Patterns of Bureaucratic Behavior

The study of large-scale public bureaucracies has been significantly influenced by Max Weber's effort to characterize an official hierarchy as an ideal-type organization capable of maintaining legal rationality in social relationships.[11] Weber assumed perfectly obedient officials acting in relation to calculable rules of law in the context of a fully consistent and complete legal system. If such assumptions do not hold, patterns of behavior in large-scale public bureaucracies may depart radically from Weber's ideal-type analysis.

Gordon Tullock, in *The Politics of Bureaucracy*, assumes instead that public bureaucracies will be composed of ambitious public employees interested in advancing their career opportunities.[12] Since promotions depend upon the actions of superiors, Tullock assumes that subordinates will advance information that is favorable to their

---

[10] Joseph L. Sax, *Defending the Environment* (New York: Alfred A. Knopf, 1971), develops the concept of public trust in relation to the interest of a citizen in a public property.

[11] Max Weber, "Bureaucracy," in H. H. Genth and C. Wright Mills, eds., *From Max Weber: Essays in Sociology* (New York: Oxford University Press, 1946), pp. 196-244.

[12] Gordon Tullock, *The Politics of Bureaucracy* (Washington, D. C.: Public Affairs Press, 1965).

career and repress information that is unfavorable. As a consequence he would expect the information forwarded to superiors to be systematically biased. Decisions will, as a consequence, be based upon biased or distorted information. He would thus expect large-scale bureaucracies to be subject to substantial error-proneness.

This filtering process can also be expected to occur in communicating commands downward through any extended hierarchy. Those at the top will be able to exercise only minimal control over those providing services to people in schools, clinics, offices or on the street. As a consequence, Tullock expects street-level public servants to engage in a bureaucratic free enterprise to maximize their own net welfare potential. Such bureaucratic free enterprise may include either implicit or explicit bribery, graft and corruption. Tullock's analysis of the effect of bureaucratic command structures leads to quite different conclusions from those derived by Max Weber. Traditional reformers advocating consolidation rarely consider the possibility that public bureaucracies may have built-in tendencies toward distortions of information, frustration of management controls and failure in performance. The agenda for the future needs to give critical attention to the performance of large-scale public bureaucracies.

Weber's theory of bureaucracy and Tullock's theory of bureaucracy need to be used to see which best explains observable patterns of behavior. Structural variations in different bureaucratic systems might then be examined to compare performances under those varying structural conditions. If neighborhood governments are introduced to provide for some public services within neighborhoods of center cities, will that change in structure lead to modifications in the patterns of behavior of old-line city agencies? Can rivalry among public service agencies enhance efficiency? Answers to these questions can only be developed as patterns of bureaucratic behavior are examined under varying conditions. We need to be as much concerned with the logic of corruption as with a logic of ideal forms.

The Relationships of Officials, Professionals and Citizen-Clients

In modern societies, services based upon highly specialized bodies of knowledge are made available through persons who engage in specialized professions and occupations. The value of these professions and occupations exists precisely because they possess specialized information and skills that are not available to others. Users of

105

professional services are thus always at a disadvantage in judging the performance of professionals.

Where professional services are rendered to individuals who themselves enjoy the benefit of that service, market conditions can prevail and individuals are free to choose from among those who make their services available. Medicine, law and engineering have been among the professions which are rendered primarily under market conditions.

The practice of many other professions, however, is associated with the provision of public services which individuals use by virtue of their being provided publicly or collectively. Military services, for example, are based upon highly specialized professional training, but such services are usually rendered through organizations with highly developed command structures. Similarly, police services, welfare services, educational services and many health services may be provided through public agencies organized to render professional services as a public service.

Many professions have also become highly organized in efforts to promote and regulate the interest of those within a particular profession. Professional associations develop rules of conduct applicable to professional practice and acquire the authority to admit, regulate and terminate persons associated with the practice of that profession.

The relationship of officials, professional public servants and citizen clientele is a sensitive problem in a democratic society. All public service agencies assign extraordinary authority to officials who are capable of exercising coercive sanctions to overcome holdout problems. One source of potential conflict thus arises from the political authority exercised by officials as against the specialized competence and authority of the professional practitioner. When, for example, should a lawyer working for a public agency acquiesce in obeying the command of a superior if he considers that command to be unlawful? Will he be criminally liable for obstructing justice if he engages in efforts to cover up unlawful actions by superiors? Will he be potentially subject to disbarment from his profession for such actions? Autonomous professional practice and bureaucratic command structures are not congenial associates.

This problem is compounded by the circumstance that both public officials and professional public servants may be quite insensitive to the discrete interests and problems of citizen-constituents or citizen-clients. Public officials are likely to identify their interests with majority coalitions and to presume that majority votes provide the basic justification to guide their decisions. Professionals who have access to governmental authority to impose their preferences upon the public may find it easy to adopt a Platonic perspective that they "know" what is good for those whom they regard as "laymen." Citizens may find that neither elected officials nor professional public servants are concerned with the particular problems of public life that citizens share with one another.

We can expect the relationships of officials, professional public servants and citizen-clients to call for careful attention on the agenda of future urban problems. Proposals for structural changes in the organization of urban systems of government will need to be carefully assessed with regard to their effect upon official, professional employee and citizen-client relationships. Will consolidation of urban governments lead to increasing frustration for professional public servants? Will this frustration be accompanied by increased unionization of the public service? Will increased unionization be accompanied by work stoppages, strikes or the special form of public service slowdown known as "working according to rule"? Will such actions accelerate the degradation of the conditions of urban life? Or, conversely, will a multiplicity of jurisdictions provide professional public servants with career opportunities among competing school districts, police forces, hospitals and welfare agencies so that individuals can seek a reasonable fit between their professional aspirations and their conditions of employment? Will such market conditions enable professional public servants to derive some of the benefits associated with the market-oriented "free" professions?[13]

These are important issues deserving a high place on the agenda for the future of urban areas. John Dewey once observed that "the man who wears the shoe knows best that it pinches and where it pinches even if the expert shoemaker is the best judge of how the trouble is to be remedied."[14] The practice of a profession among public servants needs to be informed by the preferences and aspirations of their citizen-clients. In turn, the performance of professional public servants can best be judged by whether their advice and practice improves the well-being of their citizen-clients. If not, public service can become public exploitation.

---

[13] Mark Sproule-Jones, "Toward a Theory of Public Employment" (Ph.D. dissertation, Indiana University, 1970).

[14] John Dewey, *The Public and Its Problems* (New York: Henry Holt and Company, 1927), p. 207. This observation is also attributed to Marsilio da Padua, a fourteenth century Italian political theorist.

New Research Strategies

Research on problems of urban government depends upon a critical awareness of the different theoretical perspectives that can be used in analyzing those problems. Every theoretical perspective is based upon logical inferences which can be derived from implicit or explicit assumptions. The reformers advocating metropolitan consolidation use a theoretical perspective which *explains* the consequences which will follow from different structural arrangements. Public choice analysts use a fundamentally different theoretical structure for inferential reasoning and arrive at an explanation which anticipates consequences contradictory to consolidationist expectations on several critical issues.

Contradictory conclusions provide unique research opportunities. Contending theorists can sharpen their analytical tools to derive researchable hypotheses which will permit empirical evidence to be arrayed in relation to those contradictions. Empirical research can then be used to provide evidence in relation to the contending explanations. If the weight of evidence strongly supports one explanatory theory over another explanatory theory, the study of urban government can be advanced as a scientific endeavor. Science depends upon being able to sort out concepts and ideas and build upon those with the greater explanatory capabilities.

As a consequence of the unique opportunity afforded by the existence of contradictory conclusions, we anticipate that the closing decades of the twentieth century will be marked by exciting new developments in political theory and in research methodologies for the study of urban government. We expect these developments to contribute new concepts which will also be used in the design of new experiments in urban government. "It is ideas, not vested interests, which are dangerous for good or evil."[15]

---

[15] John Maynard Keynes, *The General Theory of Employment, Interest and Money* (New York: Harcourt, Brace and World, Inc., 1936), pp. 383-384.

SUGGESTIONS FOR FURTHER INQUIRY

Readers interested in following up ideas presented in this monograph will find sufficient references in the text and footnotes to provide a start into most of the topics covered here. As an additional aid to further inquiry, we have selected for special mention a few works dealing with each topic area.

Readers interested in the relationship between thought and action will find three paperbacks especially interesting. One is Thomas Kuhn's *The Structure of Scientific Revolutions* (University of Chicago Press, 2nd edition, 1970). While Kuhn focuses on the physical sciences his study brings out the problem of examining events from different perspectives or approaches. Another book with a similar thrust, but with a direct focus on ways of thinking about patterns of public organization is Vincent Ostrom's *The Intellectual Crisis in American Public Administration* (University of Alabama Press, 1973). In this study, Ostrom compares the traditional public administration perspective, which is closely related to the reform tradition proposing consolidation, and the approaches used by public choice analysts and traditional works in American democratic theory. For a closer look at the approach used by Alexander Hamilton and James Madison in *The Federalist* to explain the design of the American political system see Vincent Ostrom's *The Political Theory of a Compound Republic* (Center for the Study of Public Choice, Virginia Polytechnic Institute and State University, Blacksburg, Virginia, 1971).

Recent representative statements from the reform tradition proposing consolidation include the Committee for Economic Development's *Modernizing Local Government* (1966) and *Reshaping Government in Metropolitan Regions* (1970). The latter indicates a potential compromise position with the reformers advocating decentralization. Two of the better statements of the reform position advocating decentralization are Milton Kotler's *Neighborhood Government: The Local Foundations of Political Life* (Bobbs-Merrill, 1969) and Alan Altshuler's *Community Control: The Black Demand for Participation in Large American Cities* (Pegasus, 1970). Of the two, Altshuler provides a more careful analysis of the pros and cons of decentralization.

Bridging the decentralist position and the public choice approach is de Tocqueville's *Democracy in America*. In de Tocqueville one can see a concern for the vitality of small political communities, as well as a way of thinking that is similar to *The Federalist* and the public choice approach. The most systematic presentation of the public choice approach to urban government is Robert Bish's *The Public Economy of Metropolitan Areas* (Markham, 1971). For a public choice analysis of large-scale bureaucratic organization and individual behavior within bureaucratic settings see Gordon Tullock's *The Politics of Bureaucracy* (Public Affairs Press, 1965).

Much work has been done on big city school systems. Good critiques and analyses of big city school systems from the decentralist perspective are contained in works by Marilyn Gittell, among which are *Educating an Urban Population* (Sage, 1967). One of the best surveys of research in education is presented in Harvey Averch, et al., *How Effective Is Schooling: A Critical Review and Synthesis of Research Findings*, prepared for the President's Commission on School Finance and published by the Rand Corporation (1972). Anyone interested in what is known about the effectiveness of schooling will find this volume useful.

Readers interested in the provision of police services will find studies by Albert J. Reiss, Jr., *The Police and the Public* (Yale University Press, 1971); Jerome Skolnick, *Justice Without Trial: Law Enforcement in Democratic Society* (Wiley, 1966); and Elinor Ostrom, William Baugh, Richard Guarasci, Roger Parks and Gordon Whitaker, *Community Organization and the Provision of Police Services* (Sage Professional Papers in Administrative and Policy Studies, 03-001, 1973) helpful. The Ostrom analysis tests hypotheses which permit comparison of the reform tradition recommending consolidation and the public choice approach as these relate to the provision of police services. Readers interested in fire protection and innovation in public services will find Roger Ahlbrandt's *Municipal Fire Protection Services: Comparison of Alternative Organization Forms* (Sage Professional Papers in Administrative and Policy Studies, 03-002, 1973) to be a useful case study which also compares traditional and public choice approaches.

Studies which deal with different aspects of intergovernmental relations include Robert Warren's *Government in Metropolitan Regions: A Reappraisal of Fractionated Political Organization* (Institute of Governmental Affairs, University of California, Davis, 1966). Warren treats the development of public sector organization in Southern California, with special reference to the development of the Lakewood Plan and intergovernmental contracting at the local level. Selma Mushkin and Joseph Cotton provide a good history and analysis of federal grant programs in *Sharing Federal Funds for State and Local Needs* (Praeger, 1969); and Frances Fox Piven and Richard Cloward provide an excellent study of joint federal-state-local government interactions in the provision of welfare services in *Regulating the Poor: The Functions of Public Welfare* (Pantheon, 1971).

In reading different materials on urban government, every person needs to give critical attention to the fact that there are different ways of thinking about patterns of human organizations. Since early childhood most of us have been aware of the fact that geographers and navigators have variously viewed the earth as being flat and as being round. The issue was only settled in the early sixteenth century. Similar differences have existed among astronomers about the relative movement of the earth, the sun and other planets and stars. The same type of problem exists in the study of human organizations. Here the question concerns the relationships of people to one another and to something that we call "government."

Each person is ultimately required to think through for himself the essential logic that applies to structure of human organizations. He can evaluate reform proposals only when he can *predict* the consequences of such proposals both in terms of potential benefits and potential costs. His ability to predict consequences depends upon his capacity to draw conclusions from a structure of inferential reasoning. The presumptions that he uses will affect his conclusions in the same way that Columbus derived the conclusion that he could reach the East by sailing west.

We hope that this monograph will begin to open new vistas for understanding urban government. If we can develop a better level of comprehension about the essential structure of urban societies, then we should be in a position to make more effective diagnostic assessments of urban social pathologies and formulate more appropriate proposals for reform.

Cover and design: Pat Taylor